Algorithms for Mutual Exclusion

MIT Press Series in Scientific Computation
Dennis Gannon, editor

Algorithms for Mutual Exclusion   M. Raynal

Translated by
D. Beeson

The MIT Press
Cambridge, Massachusetts

First MIT Press edition, 1986

English translation © 1986 by NORTH OXFORD ACADEMIC
Publishers Ltd.

Original edition published under the title *Algorithmique du
parallélisme* by Dunod informatique, France. © 1984 Bordas,
Paris.

Published in Great Britain by
NORTH OXFORD ACADEMIC Publishers Limited
a subsidiary of Kogan Page Limited
120 Pentonville Road
London N1 9JN

Printed in Great Britain

Library of Congress Cataloging in Publication Data
Raynal, M.
    Algorithms for mutual exclusion.

    Translation of: Algorithmique du parallélisme.
    Bibliography: p.
    Includes index.
    1. Parallel processing (Electronic computers)
    2. Electronic data processing – Distributed processing.
    3. Algorithms.   I. Title.
    QA76.5.R38513   1986   001.64   85-7916
ISBN 0-262-18119-3

Contents

Series Foreword

It is often the case that the periods of rapid evolution in the physical sciences occur when there is a timely confluence of technological advances and improved experimental technique. Many physicists, computer scientists and mathematicians have said that such a period of rapid change is now under way. We are currently undergoing a radical transformation in the way we view the boundaries of experimental science. It has become increasingly clear that the use of large-scale computation and mathematical modeling is now one of the most important tools in the scientific and engineering laboratory. We have passed the point of viewing the computer as a device for tabulating and correlating experimental data; we now regard it as a primary vehicle for testing theories for which no practical experimental apparatus can be built. For example, NASA scientists speak of 'numerical' wind tunnels, and physicists experiment with the large-scale structure of the universe completely by computer simulation.

The major technological change accompanying this new view of experimental science is a blossoming of new approaches to computer architecture and algorithm design. By exploiting the natural parallelism in scientific applications, new computer designs show the promise of major advances in processing power. When coupled with the current biennial doubling of memory capacity, supercomputers are on their way to becoming the laboratories of much of modern science. In addition, we are seeing a major trend toward distributing operating systems over a network of a powerful and perhaps inhomogenous, set of processors. The idea of being able to make diverse computing resources cooperate on the solution of a large problem is most exciting to the scientist whose application is part numerical, part symbolic, manages a massive data base, and outputs complex graphics.

In this series we hope to focus on the effect these changes are having on the design of both scientific and systems software. In particular, we plan to highlight many major new trends in the algorithms and the associated programming and software tools that are being driven by the new advances in computer architecture. Of course, the relation between algorithm design and computer architecture is symbiotic. New views on the structure of physical processes demand new computational models, which then drive the design of new machines. We can expect progress in this area for many years, as our understanding of the emerging science of concurrent computation deepens.

As most computer scientists realize, distributed, concurrent hardware systems represent the future of our interaction with the computers. The contemporary vision of having a thousand processors and work stations networked into a system with vast cumulative resources has captivated both industry and academia. Unfortunately, there is much more to making this a reality than just hooking the hardware together. Problems such as the synchronization of distributed concurrency, distribution of work among processors, and mantaining the integrity of a dynamic, distributed file system are numerous enough to keep a generation of scientists busy.

In *Algorithms for Mutual Exclusion*, Michel Raynal presents a unified view of the algorithms associated with mutual exclusion in concurrent systems. He considers both classical shared memory systems as well as network-based concurrency. The problems and solutions presented in this book must become part of the working knowledge of anyone seriously interested in building concurrent systems.

Dennis B. Gannon

Foreword

Constant progress in technology (in particular microprocessors and local area networks) and in programming methodology (using languages of the Ada type) is increasingly opening up computer systems as a field of research, traditionally the preserve of 'initiates', to applications designers and implementors. There are many problems involved in the design of such systems, such as the management of common memories and memories local to the various processors, the allocation of physical and virtual resources defined within the system, and concurrency protection and management. It is primarily issues of concurrency that are becoming increasingly critical. Mechanisms for the management of processes and their concurrency must often be implemented within a genuinely parallel framework, as in multiprocessor systems with or without common memory.

There is one fundamental problem that stands out from all those involved in controlling parallelism: mutual exclusion. The issue here is one of ensuring that it is possible, given a number of parallel programs, to limit their parallelism at certain points in their execution: as one program enters a particular zone of code it must exclude the others. It is this question, mutual exclusion, and its expression in algorithms that we shall consider in this book. We shall not therefore be concerned with systems design as a whole (the interested reader should consult works such as 'Crocus', *'Systèmes d'exploitation des ordinateurs'*, or 'Cornafion', *'Systèmes informatiques répartis'*) but with a particular systems component which is becoming increasingly important in their definition.

This book is divided into four parts. The first (Chapter 1) introduces the problems associated with controlling parallelism, following a deliberately didactic approach; we shall discuss mutual exclusion, deadlock and data coherence in turn. The second part (Chapters 2 and 3) describes algorithms (Chapter 2) and statements (Chapter 3) to implement mutual exclusion in a centralized framework (i.e. via access to a common memory). The third part (Chapters 4 and 5) deals with distributed algorithms for mutual exclusion. Chapter 4 will be concerned with solutions based on state variables, and Chapter 5 will describe algorithms based on message communication, the kind of protocols needed for implementation of exclusion on a network. The final part (Chapter 6) will consider original software approaches to two control problems. Although there are some cross-references, chapters can be read independently of each other.

This book is intended for computer scientists interested in the design, construction and implementation of centralized or distributed computer systems, where by 'computer systems' we mean systems as different as operating systems, database systems, document or business management systems, real-time systems, process control systems, etc. It should be of value to engineers, who will find that it contains an inventory of algorithms which are generally scattered through the specialist literature, and are sometimes difficult to track down. All the algorithms are presented in the same way: underlying principles and assumptions, the algorithm itself, proof of its valid operation with respect to expected behaviour, and comments on its structure and efficiency. From this point of view, the book is a collection of algorithms on a particular subject, of a kind that is common, for sequential programming, in works on sorting, automata and fundamental data structure. The book is also intended for students at Masters level and above, for trainee engineers in computer science and for researchers who would like to become more closely acquainted with the systems design field. Teachers will find that it contains useful supplementary material, because of the approach and the analytic point of view adopted, to standard survey or design textbooks, and could treat it as a collection of exercises on the subject of mutual exclusion. This is, in fact, a textbook on algorithms for parallel processing.

Any corrections pointed out by readers to errors we may have made will be gratefully received.

Description language and notation

The language used to describe these algorithms is a 'Pascal-style' language. We shall be essentially concerned with the basic data types: integers, scalars and Booleans; and traditional control structures: conditions, iterations, etc., where the end of a statement is explicitly given mr *if ... endif, do ... enddo*, etc. Any possible ambiguities in the interpretation of control structures are avoided by using the construction *begin ... end* to delimit processes. Assignment is shown using the sign ←.

An active delay is expressed using loops in which the statement *nothing* is used for the activity associated with waiting. The statement *wait* is used for waiting whether it is passive or active. In the latter case it is a shorthand form for which the semantics is:

> *wait C = while ⌐ C do nothing enddo*

The general format used to describe algorithms is as follows:

> < *prelude* >;
> < *critical section* >;
> < *postlude* >;

the $<$ *prelude* $>$ and $<$ *postlude* $>$ sections make up the protocol that processes must follow to enter and leave the critical section. Those parts of a process that do not include the critical section or the protocol make up the non-critical part.

Set and logical notation will sometimes be used to make writing easier. On sets we therefore have the following equivalent notations:

> *for* $i \neq j$, $i \in 1..n$ *do* .. $\equiv$ *for* i *from* 1 *to* $j - 1$, *from* $j + 1$ *to* n *do* ...

> *wait* $(\forall\ i \in 1..n : a) \equiv$
> *wait* $(a, 1 \wedge a, 2 \wedge ... \wedge a, n)$

We shall use conventional symbols with Boolean expressions:

> $\daleth$: not
> $\vee$: or
> $\wedge$: and
> $\forall$: for all
> $\exists$: there exists

Preface

Over the past 20 years, the 'mutual exclusion phenomenon' has emerged as one of the best paradigms of the difficulties associated with parallel or distributed programming.

It must be stressed at the outset that the implementation of a mutual exclusion mechanism is a very real task facing every designer of operating systems.

Even applications programmers must take a certain interest in the question, because they will have to use services provided by computer systems built around several processing units, or even several computers linked by a network. The problem is simple enough to state: what we have to do is to define fundamental operations that make it possible to resolve conflicts resulting from several concurrent processes sharing the resources of a computer system. The whole complex structure of synchronization and communication between the elements of a parallel or distributed system depends on the existence of such operations. Algorithms solving this problem are generally made up of only a dozen or so lines of code and contain only trivial assignment instructions. Parallelism, however, makes it difficult to understand their behaviour and to analyse their properties, such as avoidance of deadlock or fair conflict resolutions.

Given both the practical importance and the inherent difficulty of the problem, it is not at all surprising that a vast number of works have been published on the subject. What Michel Raynal offers here is the most important results of all this research.

Michel Raynal's aim is not merely to produce a catalogue of the various algorithms found in scientific journals or conference papers, but to provide us with a remarkable survey of the field. All the algorithms have been rewritten in a single language and restructured so as to make them easy to understand and compare. The presentation of these algorithms systematically stresses the principles guiding their design, provides arguments to prove their validity and gives quantitative data allowing their assessment. This is, as far as we know, a unique book on the subject, opening up a vast field of research which is both firmly based and highly complex: algorithms for parallel or distributed control.

There is no doubt that this is a work that must be regarded as indispensable in the library of teachers, researchers or engineers working in this field, who will use it to illustrate a lecture, launch new research or solve specific concrete problems.

Gérard Roucairol
(University of Paris-Sud)

Chapter 1

The nature of control problems in parallel processing

1.1. Processes and their interactions

The need for the control of a set of parallel processes is a consequence of the many problems associated with their management. Responsibility for this control is left to what is generally called a *system*: an operating system, a data base management system, a real time system, etc., depending on the purpose for which it is constructed.

The concept of a process is used both to express the activity associated with users of the system and the internal structure of the system itself. A number of educational works such as Crocus (1975), Shaw (1974), Peterson and Silberschatz (1983), or Lister (1979), discuss the concept and make its importance clear, illustrating it by means of examples.

In this chapter we shall start by specifying the interactions within a set of parallel processes (Section 1.1), after which we shall examine the nature of problems associated with these interactions (Section 1.2). The search for solutions to these problems has led to the emergence of algorithms of a new kind, which we call algorithms for parallel processing. The rest of this work is devoted to a study of these algorithms from the point of view of mutual exclusion.

1.1.1. The process concept

The process concept was first introduced into information systems in order to highlight the differences between a program as text (written in a certain language) and the execution of this program on a processor. Since then, the concept has been the subject of much study, leading to its more formal definition (Horning and Randell 1973). A major development was its introduction into programming languages (Wulf et al. 1971). This occurred in response to two factors. First there was the influence of technology. The concept of a process to express the idea of an activity (and which can therefore be used to structure the overall activity of a system formed from elementary activities corresponding to the different parts of the machine) has become an indispensable tool with the appearance of multiprocessors and computer

1

networks (whatever their size). If we are to make satisfactory use of such machines, it is absolutely necessary to be able to master the different activities taking place within them.

At the same time, research into programming methodology (structured programming (Dijkstra 1968, Dahl et al. 1972, Hoare 1972, Brinch Hansen 1973), programming theory, etc., showed that in order to solve a problem it was necessary to adopt an approach based on successive refinements and which applied the principle of abstraction, by which we mean that at a given level we consider only the function offered at that level independently of the way in which it is implemented. This research led to the introduction into programming languages of the concepts of processes and abstract types. The former, as we have already pointed out, is the expression within the language of the idea of an activity [i.e. of an active object (Brinch Hansen 1975, 1978, Hoare 1978)] ; the latter expresses the idea of data that the program can manipulate [i.e. the idea of a passive object (Hoare 1974, Liskov et al. 1977, Wirth 1977)].

In this way processes gradually became familiar objects to all program designers: a program would no longer always be seen (implicitly) as a single process, but could be explicitly expressed as a set of processes whatever the purpose of the program, whether implementing a system (i.e. an interface between a machine and users) or a particular application.

It is interesting that the concept of a coroutine, which makes it possible to decompose a program into a certain number of processes of which only one is active at any given moment, was introduced as early as 1963 to deal with a particular class of applications: compilers structured as several processes communicating data to each other in a 'pipeline' fashion (Conway 1963). As at that time the concept of a process did not exist in programming languages, it was up to the programmer to use both a given language and the tools provided by the system to assist in the production of software to obtain the desired behaviour. The introduction of this concept into a language makes it possible to leave all this work to the compiler; the program designer need then only concern himself with the expression of a solution to his problem in the language in question.

In the rest of our discussion we shall assume the principle that a program should be structured in terms of parallel processes whatever the techniques used for producing the program: parallel languages or sequential languages plus production tools. A fundamental question is then immediately raised: what are the interactions between processes themselves?

1.1.2. The criterion of mutual awareness

In order to reply to this question we shall consider two criteria. Like any criteria designed to distinguish absolutely between classes, ours will be to some extent arbitrary; their value lies in the 'didactic' classification that they allow for the various problems associated with control. The criteria are independent of the number of processes n (where $n > 2$) and of the level at which these processes are viewed (applications, systems).

The first criterion concerns the extent to which a process is aware of the environment (made up of other processes) with which it interacts.

Criterion 1: What degree of awareness do processes have of each other?

This criterion allows us to define two classes of processes:

C_1: processes unaware of each other

C_2: processes aware of each other.

The second class may itself be broken down into two subclasses:

C_{21}: processes indirectly aware of each other (e.g. because they use a shared object)

C_{22}: processes explicitly aware of each other (and which therefore have communication primitives available to them).

These different degrees of awareness that processes have of each other lead to different relationships between them:

R_1: competition

R_{21}: cooperation by sharing

R_{22}: cooperation by communication.

COMPETITION

In this case the processes are totally unaware of the existence of other processes: they come into conflict for the use of objects which they must leave in the same state as they found them, precisely because, as each is unaware of the existence of the others, if an object is unique, it must be the same for all of them. The objects involved in such conflicts generally make up what is known as the system resources. A *resource* is usually a model of a device (memory, peripheral, CPU, clock, etc.). The objects are not modified by the processes but they are indispensable to their operation — their role is analogous to catalysts in chemistry, as opposed to substances that undergo transformation; as is the case of catalysts when writing chemical equations, resources do not generally appear in the statement expressing a process. Synchronization rules aimed at resolving the problems associated with physical constraints must be defined so that competition between processes can take place without leading to difficulties.

Comment

Competitive interactions affect all processes executing on a given computer. To avoid them altogether it is necessary to provide more resources than there are processes that might need them at any given time, so that they can be allocated in such a way as to avoid conflict. However, this number is unknown and it is impossible to create physical resources dynamically. Competitive relationships are therefore the 'minimal' relationships between processes.

COOPERATION BY SHARING

Here, processes interacting with each other know there are other processes, without being explicitly aware of them. This is what happens, for example, with variables shared between different processes in the system or a data base: processes (or transactions) use and update the data base without reference to other processes, but know that they might be using or updating the same data.

Two read operations, for example, on a single data base may lead to different results, depending on whether or not another process has been writing to the data base. We are no longer dealing with resources that have to be allocated, but with shared data that the processes may transform. The processes must cooperate in ensuring that the data base they share is properly managed. We are dealing here with data-oriented systems, and the control mechanisms implemented must ensure that the data shared remains coherent.

Comment

Cooperative and competitive interactions between processes are by no means mutually exclusive. On the contrary: shared data by way of which processes cooperate with each other are held in resources over which the same processes will come into conflict. Synchronization rules must therefore not only sort out conflicts of access but also guarantee the coherence of the data accessed.

Within the terms of a single problem for which a layered solution has been proposed using processes, cooperative interactions at any one level may well correspond to competitive interactions at another level and vice versa. This contradicts nothing in what we are saying: we are concerned with classifying types and relationships independently of the level at which we are making our observations.

COOPERATION BY COMMUNICATION

In the first two cases above, the environment of a process does not contain the other processes, and interactions between them are always indirect. In the first case they were sharing devices without knowing it, and in the second they were sharing values. In this case, however, every process has an environment that contains names of other processes with which it may explicitly exchange data. Each process no longer has its own particular aim, but participates in a common goal which links the whole set of processes. We are dealing here with what are known as message systems, or systems of communicating processes; these systems are characterized by the presence of message transmission and reception primitives. These primitives may be provided by languages containing the appropriate linguistic constructions in their definitions [e.g. CSP (Hoare 1978) or Ada (Ichbiah et al. 1983)], they may be constructed by the programmer in a language that does not itself contain them but which does make tools available for their construction [e.g. concurrent Pascal (Brinch and Hansen 1975)], or they may be provided by a system kernel accessible to applications programs.

Comment

Access primitives and the rules governing their use are affected by the distinction we have drawn between cooperation by sharing and by communication. In cooperation by sharing, processes are unaware of each other and their cooperation primitives are the operations *read* and *write* defined on an object, and the access rule may be formally described by:

$$(read + write)^*$$

In cooperation by communication, the cooperation primitives provided are the operations *send* and *receive*, and for a pair of communicating processes we have a communication rule which we can formally describe by:

$$(send \, . \, receive)^*$$

There are cases (languages or systems) where processes are not explicitly aware of each other and use the *send* and *receive* operations all the same; under such circumstances these operations are addressed to an object of the port type (Balzer 1971, Mitchell et al. 1978) or of the communication channel type (Ambler et al. 1977). As it is not our aim to produce a classification of languages (the interested reader should consult Le Guernic and Raynal 1980), we shall only consider the two major cooperation classes (sharing/ communication), and these cases obviously belong in the latter class.

1.1.3. The corresponding criterion of mutual influence

Having used the criterion of mutual awareness to make a first, rough division of the interactions between processes into two major classes — competitive and cooperative — we can now attempt to refine our analysis by asking a second question, which will allow us to come more closely to grips with the problems posed by these kinds of relations between processes.

Criterion 2: *When processes interact competitively or cooperatively, what is the influence that the behaviour of one will have on the behaviour of others?*

In the case of competition, there is no exchange of information between processes — each has its own code and consequently the results of one process cannot be affected by the actions of others. On the other hand, the behaviour of one may be affected by the other: if there is competition between two processes for a single resource, then one will have to wait for the other to finish before using the resource. Thus, one process will have been slowed down by the other. Ultimately, it is possible for a process to be denied access to the resource indefinitely, in which case it would never terminate, and would give no result (a situation similar to that of a sequential program trapped in a loop). With cooperative interactions, a process may directly infuence another's results by means of the exchange of information.

In other words, the two cases may be distinguished by the extent to which the partial correctness of a process is independent of that of the others.

1.2. Control problems

In this section we shall examine the various problems associated with interactions between processes. To do so, we will use simple models which make the problems easy to grasp.

1.2.1. Competition between n processes for one resource

Consider the case of n processes in conflict for access to a single non-sharable resource. As the resource can only be used by a single process at a time, we shall call it a *critical resource* and it will be used in a *critical section* of the process. It will therefore be necessary to bracket the use of this resource by a protocol made up of two parts, concerned with acquiring and releasing the resource, which ensure that the resource R is used by only one process P_i:

> *acquisition protocol*   *written*: (R
>
> *< use of the resource*
> *in the critical section >* CS
>
> *release protocol*   )R

This protocol guarantees what is generally known as mutual exclusion: if, while the resource is being used by a process P_i, another process executes its acquisition protocol, that protocol must delay it until P_i has executed its release protocol.

Defining protocols is a complex problem — there are a number of pitfalls to avoid.

The first pitfall involves what is called *deadlock*. Consider several processes all attempting to enter their critical section to use the resource. As at most only one process may be in the critical section, one 'solution' would be to let none of them in. This is frequently the case when several people meet before a doorway (the resource). Imagine that they all follow the protocol: if I am alone, I go through; otherwise (several people are present), I let the others go first. If several people with this protocol arrive simultaneously at the doorway, they will all wait, blocking each other's access. This is *deadlock*. Although this protocol guarantees mutual exclusion — there is never more than one process using the resource at a given moment — it leads to a situation in which there is no activity by any of the processes; it must therefore be avoided at all costs. At least one of the processes wishing to reach the critical section must be capable of reaching it:

∃ *a process* P_i: *CS is reachable by* P_i

This is the property of reachability from the point of view of the critical section. Now consider the case where P_1 is in possession of the resource and P_2 and P_3 are delayed in active or passive waits mode, i.e. using or not using the processor, in their acquisition protocol. Once P_1 has executed its release protocol, the first step is to end the delay of P_2 or P_3. Let us assume that P_3 accesses the resource and that P_1, which now needs it again, executes its acquisition protocol once more. We shall then find ourselves in the following situation:

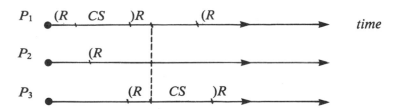

The second pitfall to avoid is a mechanism whereby the resource is again allocated to P_1 once P_3 has executed its release protocol. If, in fact, this happens, and if P_1 and P_3 make very considerable use of the resource, we may end up with the processes behaving in such a way that P_2 is indefinitely delayed in its acquisition protocol and will never access the resource. Such a situation is called *starvation*. It is naturally assumed that P_2 does not deliberately halt, i.e. that it continues to execute its acquisition protocol (unless it is in a passive waiting mode). This is called the *progress hypothesis* for processes: the execution of two consecutive instructions in an acquisition or release protocol are separated by a finite period of time — an infinite delay would correspond to the process having halted. In other words, a process may execute a protocol at any *non-zero* speed.

We also make the assumption that the use of a resource by a process takes a finite time; otherwise, of course, a process could be permanently in its critical section, excluding all other processes from the possibility of accessing the resource. This assumption concerns the use of the resource and not the protocol that governs its acquisition or release. We shall assume in what follows that these two assumptions always hold.

Different forms of process delay can be distinguished. We shall say:

(a) The delay is FIFO if processes enter their critical section in the order of their arrival.

(b) The delay is linear if a process may not enter its critical section twice while another process is waiting, i.e. there is no *a priori* order amongst the processes that are waiting, but a process that has already been through its critical section and requests permission to do so again may not jump ahead of a requesting process with which it had been waiting previously.

(c) The delay is said to be limited by $f(n)$, where n is a number of processes, if the protocol ensures that a process attempting to use the resource, and therefore executing its acquisition protocol, cannot be overtaken by more than $f(n)$ requests for use of the resource and entry to a critical section.

(d) The delay is said to be finite if, while unbounded, it is not infinite.

If the delay is finite (whether a known limit to it exists or not), starvation cannot occur: we then say that the protocol guarantees *fairness*. Any process that is attempting to enter its critical section will reach it within a finite time:

$\forall$ *processes* P_i: *CS is reachable by* P_i

This is the property of reachability from the point of view of the process; it implies the property of reachability from the point of view of the critical section.

TO SUMMARIZE:

FIFO delay $\Rightarrow$ *linear delay* $\Rightarrow$ *limited delay* $\Rightarrow$ *finite delay* $\Leftrightarrow$ non-starvation $\equiv \forall P_i$: *CS is reachable by* $P_i \Rightarrow \exists P_i$ *CS is reachable by* $P_i \equiv$ *no deadlock*

'Minimal' properties of mutual exclusion protocols

For obvious reasons, all algorithms implementing a mutual exclusion protocol must have a minimum number of properties that make them operational. Following Dijkstra (1965), we can summarize them as follows:

(a) No more than one process may be in its critical section at any one time. (This is the definition of the critical section.)

(b) If several processes are waiting to enter a critical section while no process is actually in its critical section, one of them must enter it within a finite time; i.e. the critical section is reachable.

(c) The behaviour of a process outside its critical section or of the protocol governing access to it has no influence on the mutual exclusion protocol — there is complete independence between those parts potentially involved in access conflicts and those parts that are not.

(d) There is no privileged process: the problem is solved in the same way for all of them — the solution is standardized.

Any new mutual exclusion protocol must allow for these properties. As can be seen, they say nothing of the problem of starvation. There are, in fact, cases in which starvation cannot be ruled out *a priori*, e.g. where certain repetitive processes have higher priority than others, in which case there is nothing to prevent such high-priority processes monopolizing the resource indefinitely. However, in most cases we shall attempt to define a protocol guaranteeing not only the mutual exclusion property, but also its fairness.

Comment

If a resource can be accessed by more than one process at a time, two situations may arise. If any number of processes may use the resource at the same time, competition will never become a problem. However, if the number of processes allowed access is limited to $nb < n$, the mutual exclusion protocol must be modified in such a way as to allow a maximum of nb processes to use the resource. This can be done simply by adding a counter cnb which stores the number of processes using the resource at any given time; cnb is respectively incremented or decremented in the acquisition or release protocols, and the acquisition protocol only plays its mutual exclusion role when $cnb = nb$. The same is true for the situation where access to nb identical resources under mutual exclusion takes place, governed by a single exclusion protocol.

1.2.2. Competition between *n* processes for *m* resources

We shall now extend our initial model. It contained n processes and a single resource subject to exclusive access. It allowed us not only to show that a protocol to guarantee mutual exclusion was necessary, but also to highlight problems associated with the reachability of a resource by processes: starvation and deadlock.

Let us now consider a model along the same lines, in which there are n processes and m unique resources which can only be accessed by one process at a time. Does such a change lead to any new problems?

In order to answer this question, consider two processes P_1 and P_2, two resources R_1 and R_2 subject to exclusive access, and imagine the following situation in which P_1 and P_2 are using R_1 and R_2 respectively, having made their requests for them and then obtained them. At times t_1 and t_2, P_1 and P_2 are executing their acquisition protocols for R_2 and R_1, but both processes will be blocked because the resource that each wants to use is being used by the other. We have once more, as in the case of the single resource model, reached deadlock, but here this is not a consequence of non-reachability from the point of view of the resources (a process is in fact using each of them), but is due to the mutual exclusion conditions themselves.

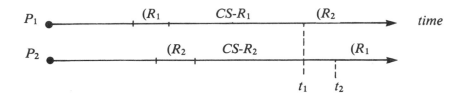

The problem that is posed in a model where n processes are in competition for the use of m resources is therefore one of deadlock. Let us examine this in more detail. By making a fundamental assumption concerning their construction, we can say that processes wanting to use resources acquire them sequentially. (This assumption is based on the fact that the exclusion mechanism provided by any hardware is based on exclusive access to one memory location at a time.) Under what conditions does deadlock arise?

(a) In the first place, there must be resources subject to exclusive access, i.e. that require a mutual exclusion protocol. A process attempting to use such a resource must await its release if it is being used by another process.

(b) For there to be mutual blocking of processes, as is shown by the example, there must be at least one process using a resource and which is waiting for another resource being used by another process.

(c) No resource has pre-emptive powers: i.e. resources are released voluntarily by processes and not obligatorily because other processes have requested them.

(d) Finally, the fundamental condition for deadlock is that there is a cycle in the graph of waiting processes. The vertices of such a graph are the processes, and there exists an edge between P_i and P_j if P_i is waiting for a resource in P_i's possession. The presence of a cycle in such a graph reveals the presence of a mutual waiting relation, i.e. deadlock.

Comment

We have in this discussion only considered resources available in a single copy and accessible only in an exclusive mode. There may, of course, be configurations in which resources have other characteristics:

— there may be a number of copies of each resource
— they may be accessible in a variety of modes.

These characteristics, although they mean that other algorithms must be used to resolve deadlock, do not alter the nature of the deadlock problem as such.

1.2.3. Cooperation between n processes by sharing m data items

As data are held on devices (resources), the problems we have been discussing — mutual exclusion, starvation, deadlock — have to be resolved for cases of cooperation by data sharing. But this raises another question: does the addition of semantics (values) to a device create new control problems? We have already seen that processes cooperating by sharing may influence each other (Section 1.1.3): they are not independent of each other with respect to partial correctness — the results obtained depend on the data shared by reading and/or writing.

Consider the simple case of n processes and a single shared data item. Apart from the fact that the successive values taken by the latter may affect the elaboration of results provided by the processes, there is nothing to distinguish this case, from the control point of view, from that of competition between n processes for access to a single common resource. Control problems (exclusion, starvation, deadlock) therefore remain the same, the only difference being that the data item may be accessed in two different modes, reading and writing, with the property that reading operations are not mutually exclusive.

Let us extend our model to consider n processes sharing m data items. Two cases may arise: individual items of data are independent of each other, or they are not. In the first case, from the point of view of controlling parallel processing, the processes compete for access to the devices (resources) on which the m data items are held, and the problems are the same as those we met above. On the other hand, if the data items depend on each other, this is no longer the case. For, in fact, the *mutual dependence relations* governing these data items [generally called *integrity constraints* (Eswaran et al. 1976)] may be infringed by the parallel execution of the processes. Take the following example. Let two items of data a and b be linked by the relation $a = b$. This relation must hold at any time the data may be observed (i.e. before and after the execution of the process: consistent states). Now consider the following two processes:

$$P_1 : a \leftarrow a + 1;$$
$$\quad\quad b \leftarrow b + 1;$$
$$P_2 : b \leftarrow 2 * b;$$
$$\quad\quad a \leftarrow 2 * a;$$

As can be seen, if the state is initially consistent, each process taken separately will leave the shared data in a consistent state. Now let us examine the following parallel execution, in which the processes respect a mutual exclusion protocol on variables a and b (our starting condition is $a = b = i$); parallelism is expressed by dovetailing the processes with each other:

$$a \leftarrow a + 1;$$
$$b \leftarrow 2 * b;$$
$$b \leftarrow b + 1;$$
$$a \leftarrow 2 * a;$$

relation $a = b$ no longer holds at the end of the execution; we have, in fact

$$a = 2(i + 1) \neq b = 2i + 1$$

We therefore have a *data coherence* control problem: we need to ensure that if processes taken in isolation respect the mutual coherence of data, their parallel execution will also respect it. It is important to realize that data coherence cannot be reduced to mutual exclusion, starvation or deadlock, as shown by the example above, which does not involve deadlock or a failure to respect mutual exclusion, but data coherence is not guaranteed.

Compared with competition for access·to n resources, cooperation by sharing mutually dependent data introduces a need for controlling data coherence with respect to dependence rules. Resources are not linked by semantic relations and the only problem is to ensure that their allocation creates no problems; when it comes to data, however, there is the additional requirement to respect their rules of mutual dependence.

1.2.4. Cooperation between n processes by message communication

Within a set of processes communicating by messages, some may enter into competition for the use of common resources, leading to problems with which we are already familiar, starvation and deadlock.

The fundamental question is the same as in the case of cooperation by shared data: does cooperation by way of message transmission and reception operations lead to new control problems? Quite apart from the underlying control requirements for process execution, there are questions to be solved at the level of the processes themselves, concerning their communication. There are various ways of organizing communication, which we will distinguish by applying the criterion: can the communication of a message lead to a process being delayed? One obvious comment must be made: because of the causality relation between transmission and reception, the message can only be received once, and reception must follow on from a corresponding transmission. This is the essential difference between message communication and cooperation by data item sharing, in which there is no such dependence relation: a data item may be read, or written, several times without having been written, or read, in the meantime. Reception may therefore potentially be blocked by the corresponding transmission. But can the reverse occur: can transmission be blocked by reception? There are three cases to consider, depending on the size of the buffer being used for communication. If it is equal to zero, the transmitting process must be blocked until the process addressed is ready to receive the message, assuming there is no loss of messages; in such cases, we speak of *rendezvous* between the two processes involved in communication. If the size t of the buffer is finite, the transmitter is not blocked while there is still free space in the buffer; on the other hand, if the buffer is full, the transmitter must wait for a receiver to consume a value and thus free a place in the buffer, which takes us back to the rendezvous position from the control point of view, although, of course, from the 'values' point of view, there is a gap of length t between the transmitted and received messages. There is therefore no difference with regard to potential blocking between a buffer of finite size and one of zero size; so far as control is concerned, we will treat the two cases together under the general heading of rendezvous (but a buffer of size $t > 0$ will allow an improvement in performance by increasing asynchronism between processes). As soon as buffer size is infinite, there is no longer any possibility of the transmitter being blocked, because there is always free space available.

In summary, reception always has the potential for delay. Although the same is true for transmission in the rendezvous case, it is no longer the case if the buffer is infinite, in which case transmission can never be blocked.

Blocking due to communication between processes can therefore occur, and deadlock is possible if several processes are attempting to communicate in an incompatible way, e.g. if two processes are each waiting for a message from the other. Deadlock of this kind differs from the type associated with competition for unique resources, as here all we have to do is to detect its occurrence. It is not a matter of defining resource allocation protocols that avoid deadlock, because deadlock cannot be caused by the inadequate control of processes but rather by the processes themselves.

Let us consider the various possibilities for deadlock. As above, we shall use a graph representing the blocking relations between processes: an edge between two processes means that one is awaiting communication, by transmission or reception, with the other. Suppose that at a given moment a process Q is attempting to communicate with one of several other possible processes $P_1 \dots P_n$. If communication cannot take place, we add edges $Q \rightarrow P_1, \dots Q \rightarrow P_n$ to the waiting graph. Does a cycle in such a graph constitute a sufficient condition for deadlock, as in the case of unique resources? The answer is no. In the present case, a process Q awaiting communication with one of several possible processes $P_1, \dots P_n$, although it may appear in a cycle of waiting processes, may well be waiting for a process that is in fact active. For Q to be deadlocked, all the processes reachable from Q within the graph must be blocked, i.e. each must have a successor in the graph.

Conditions for deadlock are therefore different in cooperation by messages and competition. This is a consequence of the fact that in the case of communication there may be multiple *ou* type waits, while in the resources case there are only simple waits, which at any one time apply to only one unique resource.

Apart from its specific risks of deadlock, communication between processes may also lead to problems of starvation. Consider three processes P_1, P_2 and P_3 which find themselves repeatedly in a situation where P_1 is attempting to communicate either with P_2 or P_3, while both P_2 and P_3 are attempting to communicate with P_1. It is then possible that P_1 and P_2 will communicate repeatedly, while P_3 cannot establish communication with P_1 and remains blocked. There is no deadlock between P_3 and P_1, as P_1 remains active, but P_3 is starved. If this is to be avoided, the protocols implemented for communication must ensure fairness.

Comment

There are languages that contain the process concept and provide primitives for message communication in which no assumption is made about the degree of fairness that the implementation of the mechanisms provided might guarantee: it is up to the processes themselves to contain the appropriate guarantees in the body of their code. This is the case of languages such as CSP (Hoare 1978) and Ada (Ichbiah et al. 1983), in which if several communications are possible at any given time, one is selected arbitrarily. This we shall call *non-determinism*.

The final problem associated with communication is linked to the underlying control of process execution: protocols that implement communications must ensure that a communication takes place within a finite time from the moment at which it becomes possible. A similar problem was met in the case of competition, the reachability condition applied to communication considered as a resource. There is, however, a fundamental difference. Whereas it is possible for the use of several resources to overlap, which, as we saw, led to the problem of deadlock, communications are atomic: the process can engage in no other action between the beginning and end of message transmission or reception — there cannot therefore be deadlock at this level. Communication implementation protocols therefore do not have to resolve deadlock problems, but have simply to ensure that they add none to processes whose definition avoids them.

1.3. Parallel processes, centralized or distributed

We are only concerned here with algorithms for controlling parallel processes, whether the environment in which they execute is centralized or distributed. Consequently, we shall define these terms to suit our particular requirements. Although one can be simulated using the other, we shall use the word *centralized* where control algorithms are based on the existence of a central memory that all processes can access simultaneously for reading or writing. We shall use the word *distributed* where there is no common memory, each process having a local memory to which it has sole access. In the latter case, each process can obtain values from other processes or send values to them only by way of messages. However, in most cases we shall assume that a process can read the local memories of other processes but never modify them. It is possible that by the time one process obtains the value of a variable from another, that value will have undergone further change: in a distributed system, there is no global point of view.

This is all we need to say for the purposes of our discussion. Readers interested in going further into the concepts involved in centralized or distributed processes should consult Peterson and Silberschatz (1983) or Alford et al. (1985) respectively.

The rest of this work will deal with the problem of mutual exclusion and its resolution in centralized or distributed contexts.

Chapter 2

The mutual exclusion problem in a centralized framework: software solutions

2.1. Introduction

There are several ways to solve the problems posed by implementation of mutual exclusion in a centralized framework.

Solutions will be different, depending on the level at which we approach the problem, and, indeed, at certain levels the problem may be regarded as already solved (as is the case in certain languages that provide linguistic constructions for parallelism and its control). There is, however, one constant feature: whatever the level, elementary mutual exclusion is assumed. From the point of view of the software solutions in which we are interested, this takes the form of exclusive access to the elementary storage locations provided by the memory access mechanism: several simultaneous accesses to the same location (reading and/or writing) are serialized, i.e. executed one after the other, in an order that is unknown beforehand.

VALUE OF SUCH SOLUTIONS

The algorithms we shall discuss will operate at this 'machine level', to implement protocols guaranteeing mutual exclusion. Although there are hardware solutions to the problem, there are several reasons why software solutions are worth studying.

First of all, there is what we might call the historic interest of the question. Up to 1965, the problem of whether a software solution existed at all had still to be resolved. Once one solution had been proposed, many others appeared, some of which were improvements, from the point of view of efficiency or quality (inclusion of new properties) of already existing solutions. The algorithms involved can therefore be read as something of a serial, in which each episode has its own date-line and illustrates the evolution of control algorithms for mutual exclusion, and, by extension, the changing nature of the problems that systems designers faced and the solutions they found.

Moreover, there is undoubted educational value in studying these solutions. The way in which the problem is solved varies enormously, whether in the algorithm itself or in the proof of its validity. It is, for instance, difficult to

17

improve on Peterson's algorithm (1981) in the case of two processes: the very simplicity of the solution makes any proof unnecessary. At the educational level, these solutions can therefore be used as exercises on synchronization to supplement a course on operating systems (Brinch Hansen 1973, Shaw 1974, Crocus 1975, Haberman 1976, Lister 1979, Peterson and Silberschatz 1983).

Another point, which has much in common with points already made, is that mutual exclusion is a highly topical question. There has been a rebirth of interest in the problem since the appearance of distributed structures (software or hardware) and the emergence of a constantly increasing need for reliable algorithms. We shall see in the following chapters how certain centralized solutions have been distributed to take account of new architectures or new needs.

THE FUNDAMENTAL CHARACTERISTIC OF ALGORITHMS

The common denominator of these algorithms is their centralization. They use a certain number of variables giving concrete expression to the state of the processes, and one at least of them is accessed, both for reading and for writing, by all the processes. This centralized variable will be named *turn* in all the algorithms. A fault in the memory holding this variable will cause the algorithm as a whole to break down: it is therefore a 'critical' variable, which we shall call a *shared variable*. We shall see that distributed algorithms, whether they are based on the use of state variables or on message communication, use no such variables and this is their specific characteristic.

A variable that is not shared will be called *local* to a process, and only that process may then write it or read it, or the variable may be *specific* to a process, in which case only that process may write it while all processes may read it.

2.2. Exclusion between two processes: Dekker's algorithm (1965)

In a famous paper, Dijkstra (1965) stated the constraints that any solution to the mutual exclusion problem must satisfy and gave, in didactic form, the first algorithm solving the problem for two processes. The algorithm was designed by the Dutch mathematician T. Dekker.

The stated constraints were:

(i) No assumption is made concerning the instructions or the number of processes supported by the machine, except that basic instructions such as read, write or test a memory location are executed atomically, i.e. if two such instructions are executed simultaneously, the result is equivalent to their sequential execution in an order not known beforehand.

(ii) No assumption is made about the execution speed of competing processes, except that it is non-zero.

(iii) When a process is in the non-critical section (i.e. outside the critical section or the protocol controlling it) it cannot prevent another process from entering the critical section.

(iv) It must not be possible for a process requiring access to a critical section to be delayed indefinitely.

Note that constraint (iv) expresses the reachability of the critical section (i.e. the avoidance of deadlock), which the solution must satisfy.

The solution proposed by Dekker solves the problem in the case where there are two processes; we can derive it in stages.

STAGE 1

A first approximation uses a shared variable *turn* to give the identity number of the process that may access the critical section. *Turn* will have a value of 0 or 1 and is arbitrarily initialized to one or other of these two values. When *turn* $= i$ process P_i may enter the critical section. The protocol is as follows for P_i:

> *while turn* $\neq i$ *do nothing* **enddo** ;
>
> $<$ *critical section* $>$;
>
> *turn* $\leftarrow j$;

This solution guarantees the mutual exclusion property — not more than one process may be in the critical section at any one time — but it does not respect constraint (iii): processes may only enter the critical section in succession. If we placed *turn* before P_i's active wait in order to eliminate this problem, we would obtain the solution:

> *turn* $\leftarrow i$;
>
> *while turn* $\neq$ *do nothing* **enddo** ;
>
> $<$ *critical section* $>$;
>
> *turn* $\leftarrow j$;

which does not guarantee mutual exclusion. This solution is therefore to be rejected.

STAGE 2

The problem with our first solution is that it stores the name of the process that may enter the critical section, whereas, in fact, what is needed is information on the state of each process in order to take a decision.

To obtain this information, we will replace variable *turn* by the following shared array (initialized to false):

var flag : *array* [0 .. 1] *of boolean* ;

so *flag* [*i*] = *true* means that P_i is in its critical section. The protocol for process P_i will then be:

while flag [*j*] *do nothing enddo* ;

flag [*i*] ← *true* ;

< *critical section* > ;

flag [*i*] ← *false* ;

Even though process P_i indicates its own state and tests that of P_j ($j = i + 1$ *mod* 2) in its prelude and postlude (acquisition and release protocols), this solution does not guarantee mutual exclusion in cases where P_i and P_j 'simultaneously' execute the corresponding statements, as is shown by the following sequence:

P_i *executes the* **while** *statement and finds flag* [*j*] *set to false*

P_j *executes the* **while** *statement and finds flag* [*i*] *set to false*

P_i *sets* **flag** [*i*] *to true and enters its critical section*

P_j *sets* **flag** [*j*] *to true and enters its critical section*

This solution is not therefore independent of process execution speeds.

STAGE 3

Incorrect operation in this case is a consequence of the fact that P_i can test the state of P_j before P_j has modified it. To resolve the problem, we reverse the two lines of the entry section. The protocol for P_i then becomes:

flag [*i*] ← *true* ;
while flag [*j*] *do nothing enddo* ;
< *critical section* > ;
flag [*i*] ← *false* ;

Mutual exclusion is then guaranteed, but there is another problem: if both processes advance simultaneously through their entry sections, they will block each other as each will believe that the other has entered its critical section. Constraint (iv) is therefore not respected.

STAGE 4

This problem results from the fact that when P_i sets its state it does not know the state of P_j, and in particular it does not know whether P_j is ready to set *flag* [*j*] to true. This observation leads to our adopting the following solution, in which P_i sets *flag* [i] to true to indicate its intention of entering its critical section:

> *flag* [i] ← *true*;
> **while** *flag* [j] **do** *flag* [i] ← *false*;
>   **while** *flag* [j] **do** nothing **enddo**;
>   *flag* [i] ← *true*;
>   **enddo**;
> < *critical section* > ;
> *flag* [i] ← *false*;

This solution can still lead to deadlock between the two processes if they execute at the same speed. It therefore does not respect constraints (ii) and (iv) and so must be rejected. It would appear that simply to observe the states of the processes is not sufficient to provide a solution. Use of the variable *turn* from the first stage will make it possible to sort out the 'mutual courtesy' of the processes, by imposing an order on them chosen beforehand.

DEKKER'S ALGORITHM

Dekker's algorithm is derived from this last observation. The two processes P_0 and P_1 share the following variables:

> **var** *flag* : **array** [0 .. 1] *of boolean*;
>   *turn* : 0 .. 1;

flag is initialized to false and *turn* has the value 0 or 1.

The protocol for P_i then becomes:

> *flag* [i] ← *true*;
> **while** *flag* [j] **do if** *turn* = j **then**
>   **begin**
>   *flag* [i] ← *false*;
>   **while** *turn* = j **do** nothing **enddo**;
>   *flag* [i] ← *true*;
>   **end**;
>   **endif**;
>   **enddo**;
> < *critical section* > ;
> *turn* ← j;
> *flag* [i] ← *false*;

PROOF

First, the solution respects constraint (i): the protocol contains no special statement. We have therefore only to show, without making any assumption concerning process speed [constraint (ii)], that this protocol guarantees mutual exclusion and also avoids deadlock.

Process P_i will only enter its critical section if *flag* $[j]$ is false; as only P_i may modify *flag* $[i]$, and P_i tests *flag* $[j]$ only when *flag* $[i]$ is true, it follows that when P_i enters its critical section we have: *flag* $[i] \wedge \neg$ *flag* $[j]$. Therefore the mutual exclusion property holds.

To prove critical section reachability, consider first of all the case in which a single process P_i is attempting to enter the critical section. It will find *flag* $[j]$ set to false, and enters the section without difficulty. Now consider the case where both processes are attempting to enter their critical sections and where the value of *turn* is 0 (similar reasoning applies to the case where *turn* is equal to 1). Note that the value of *turn* is modified only in the postlude. There are two possible cases. If P_1 finds *flag* $[0]$ false, it enters the critical section; if, on the other hand, it finds *flag* $[0]$ true, then P_0 will enter the critical section before P_1 within a finite time. Consider P_0: as *turn* equals 0, it will wait in its external loop for *flag* $[1]$ to be set to false (without modifying the value of *flag* $[0]$). Meanwhile, P_1 sets *flag* $[1]$ to false (and will wait in its internal loop because *turn* equals 0). At that point, P_0 will enter the critical section, which proves that deadlock is avoided.

Is there a risk of starvation in this solution? It may happen if P_i is a very fast repetitive process which, as it constantly finds *flag* $[j]$ = *false*, keeps entering its critical section, while P_j, leaving the internal loop in which it was waiting for its turn, cannot set *flag* $[j]$ to true, being prevented from doing so by P_i's reading of the variable. (It should be remembered that access to the variable takes place under mutual exclusion.) The fairness of the algorithm therefore depends on the fairness of the hardware: if the hardware is fair, P_j cannot be indefinitely prevented from updating *flag* $[j]$, even if P_i reads this value an infinite number of times.

Dekker's algorithm therefore resolves conflicts within a finite time, both from the point of view of the critical section (it will necessarily be reached if processes are attempting to enter it) and from the point of view of the processes (a process wanting to enter the critical section will be able to do so), although the latter depends on the hardware being fair. This is, in any case, an assumption that is made in all the solutions.

2.3. Generalization to *n* processes: Dijkstra's algorithm (1965)

Dijkstra (1965) generalized Dekker's solution to the case of *n* processes. As in the previous case, the solution must be symmetrical for all processes. As it was originally presented, this algorithm was weak on structure, in that it contained branches. What we shall propose is a more structured form, both at the level of control structures — iterations are used instead of branches — and at that of data structures — elements capable of taking three values are used instead of groups of Booleans, as in Peterson and Silberschatz (1983). The variables shared between the n processes P_0, ..., P_i, ..., P_{n-1} are:

> **var** *flag* : **array** $[0 .. n - 1]$ **of** (*passive*, *requesting*, *in-cs*);
>   *turn* : $0 .. n - 1$;

The elements of *flag* are initialized to *passive*, and *turn* takes some arbitrary value. We shall start by giving the protocol, and then go on to explain it and prove it. Each process P_i has an integer variable j.

> **repeat**
>   *flag* $[i]$ ← *requesting*;
>   **while** *turn* $\neq$ *i* **do if** *flag* $[turn] = passive$
>   **then** *turn* ← *i*
>   **endif**;
>   **enddo**;
>   *flag* $[i]$ ← *in-cs*;
>   *j* ← 0;
>   **while** $(j < n) \wedge (j = i \vee flag\ [j] \neq in\text{-}cs)$
>   **do** $j \leftarrow j + 1$
>   **enddo**;
>   **until** $j \geqslant n$;
>   < *critical section* >;
>   *flag* $[i]$ ← *passive*;

PROOF

In order to prove the mutual exclusion property, note that P_i can only enter its critical section when *flag* $[j] \neq in\text{-}cs$ for all values of $j \neq i$. As P_i alone can set *flag* $[i]$ ← *in-cs* and as it only tests *flag* $[j]$ after making that assignment, it follows that not more than one process may enter the critical section at any one time. Alternatively, we can reason by *reductio ad absurdum*, showing that the assumption that two processes may be in the critical section simultaneously leads to a contradiction.

To show that processes cannot block each other, we shall start with the observation that when P_i attempts to enter its critical section we have *flag* $[i]$ $\neq passive$. Moreover, *flag* $[i] = in\text{-}cs$ does not imply that *turn* $= i$; in fact, several processes may find *flag* $[turn] = passive$ and, as *turn* is a shared variable, it will contain the number of the last process to have had a value assigned to it, e.g. *i*. Processes P_j which then test *flag* $[turn]$ will therefore loop, and their variables *flag* $[j]$ will retain the value *requesting*. Now consider processes P_1, ..., P_i, ..., P_m, such that *flag* $[i] = in\text{-}cs$, and suppose that *turn* $= k$, with $l \leqslant k \leqslant m$. P_k will then enter its critical section within a finite time. The other processes P_i will leave the second internal loop with $j < n$, and return to the first loop after having carried out the assignment *flag* $[i]$ ← *requesting*. P_k may then loop round its external loop or the second internal loop (not the first, as *turn* = *k*) until the other processes have modified the value of *flag* [*i*], which they will necessarily do, owing to the assumption that processes advance — i.e. they may execute at non-zero speed; P_k will then be the only process for which *flag* [*i*] = *in-cs* and it will enter its critical section.

PROPERTIES

This solution therefore guarantees mutual exclusion and avoids deadlock; it does not, however, avoid the risk of starvation. If, in fact, a number of processes are constantly demanding entrance to their critical sections, there is nothing to stop one of these processes always being the last to modify *turn* when competing for the modification of this variable.

ANOTHER EXPRESSION

We shall now give an alternative structured expression of Dijkstra's algorithm proposed by certain authors. As it only differs by the form in which it is expressed, the properties remain the same as above (mutual exclusion, avoidance of deadlock, but risks of starvation).

The variables shared by the *n* processes P_0, ...P_i, ..., P_{n-1} are:

> *var present* : *array* [0 .. n − 1] *of boolean* ;
> > *turn* : 0 .. *n* − 1;

Array *present* is initialized to false and variable *turn* takes an arbitrary value.

The protocol for process P_i then becomes:

> *repeat*
> > *repeat present* [*i*] ← *false* ;
> > > *if turn* = 0 *then turn* ← *i* *endif* ;
> > *until turn* = *i* ;
> > *present* [*i*] ← *true* ;
> *until testp* (*i*);
> < *critical section* > ;
> *turn* ← 0;
> *present* ← *false* ;

testp is a function returning a Boolean result; the specification is as follows:

$$testp\ (i) = true \Leftrightarrow (\forall\ j \neq i: \neg\ present\ [j]) \wedge present\ [i]$$

i.e. P_i is then the only process for which the variable *present* [*i*] is set to true. In Pascal this function could be implemented by the following code:

```
function testp (i : 0 .. n − 1) : boolean;
var    j : 0 .. n;
       b : boolean;
   begin
       b := true; j := 0;
       while b and j < n do
          begin
                 b := (j = i) or not present [j] ;
                 j := j + 1;
       end;
     testp := b;
end;
```

2.4. Hyman's incorrect solution (1966)

Finding a software solution to the mutual exclusion problem became something of a challenge to computer scientists in the sixties, leading to the publication of many false solutions, including the following which was proposed by Hyman (1966).

The two processes P_0 and P_1, which compete for access to their critical sections, share the following variables:

```
var flag : array 0 .. 1 of boolean;
    turn : 0 .. 1;
```

initialized respectively to false and to some arbitrary value.

The protocol proposed for P_i is then (where $i = 0$ or 1, $j = i + 1$ *mod* 2):

```
flag [i] ← true;
while turn ≠ i do
              while flag [j] do nothing enddo;
              turn ← i;
              enddo;
< critical section > ;
flag [i] ← false;
```

It is easy to find a counter example to this 'solution'. Consider the case where *turn* equals 0 and P_1 sets *flag* [1] to true and then finds *flag* [0] set to false. P_0 will then set *flag* [0] to true, find *turn* = 0 and enter its critical section. P_1 will then assign 1 to *turn* and will also enter its critical section.

This incorrect algorithm is an interesting item for the history of science — even the *Communications of the ACM* can get it wrong — and it can be usefully cited in an educational context: this attempted solution, which set out to simplify Dijkstra's algorithm for two processes, can help clarify the qualities of a correct solution.

2.5. A fair solution: Knuth's algorithm (1966)

Dijkstra's solution, as we have seen, guarantees mutual exclusion and the reachability of the critical section, but does not avoid the risk of starvation for processes: it does not guarantee fairness. The first fair solution was proposed by Knuth (1966). It therefore respects the four constraints defined by Dijkstra and one more:

(v) A process attempting to enter its critical section will be able to do so within a finite time.

This constraint is sometimes formulated differently: there must be a limit on the number of times that other processes may enter a critical section between the moment a process submits a request to enter its own critical section and the moment it actually does so. This is a better formulation because it makes it possible to measure the maximum waiting time of a process in 'numbers of times'.

Our presentation of Knuth's protocol will use much the same notation as before. The processes share the following variables:

> *var flag* : *array* $0 .. n - 1$ *of* (*passive, requesting, in-cs*);
> *turn* : $0 .. n - 1$;

initialized to *passive* and 0 respectively; each process has a local variable j of the type $0 .. n - 1$. The protocol for process P_i is the following ($0 \leqslant i \leqslant n - 1$):

> *repeat*
>   *flag* [i] ← *requesting*;
> j ← *turn*;
>   *while* $j \neq i$ *do*
>   *if flag* [j] $\neq$ passive *then* j ← *turn*
>   *else* j ← ($j - 1$) *mod n*
>   *endif*;
>   *enddo*;
>   *flag* [i] ← *in-cs*;
> *until testd* (i);
> *turn* ← i;
> < *critical section* > ;
> *turn* ← ($i - 1$) *mod n*;
> *flag* [i] ← *passive*;

where function *testd* (i) is defined by:

> *testd* (i) = *true* ($\forall j \neq i$: *flag* [j] $\neq$ *in-cs*)
> $\wedge$ *flag* [i] = *in-cs*

and is implemented iteratively.

PROOF

This solution guarantees mutual exclusion: it is easy to show that it is impossible for *testd* (i) and *testd* (j) to be simultaneously true. It also guarantees that the critical section is reachable: if no process enters the critical section, the value of *turn* remains constant and the first process (in the cyclical order *turn*, *turn* − 1, ..., 0, n − 1, ..., *turn* + 1) attempting to enter will be able to do so.

The solution is fair, as will now be proven. For a process P_i to be incapable of reaching the critical section, which we know is in general reachable, there must be at least one other process P_j (or several) that will reach the critical section infinitely often and continually prevent P_i doing so. But this means that each time P_j executes its protocol and finds *flag* $[i]$ ≠ *passive*, the value of *turn* that it meets at the second line must have been set by a process P_k that follows P_i and precedes P_j (i.e. $i > k > j$) in the cycle: n − 1, n − 2, ..., 1, 0, n − 1 (if such a P_k does not exist, then P_i is not blocked). Since P_j continually overtakes P_i — this is the unfairness hypothesis — the effect allowing this to happen must also occur continually, i.e. P_k always enters the critical section before P_j. There must therefore be a process P'_k that follows P_i and precedes P_k, i.e. $i > k' > k$, and so on. The number of processes n is, however, finite therefore P_i must at some stage enter its critical section. Thus, the fairness of the solution is guaranteed.

We leave it as an exercise to the reader to prove that the maximum delay imposed on any process is given by the function $d(n) = 2^{n-1} - 1$ turns, where n is the number of processes, and a turn is defined as one process using its critical section. Note that the successive values of *turn* are not always consecutive.

CASE OF TWO PROCESSES

When n is very large, this algorithm is not particularly efficient. If, however, there are only two processes, it can be simplified and gives the following protocol for P_i, where index i is 0 or 1 and $j = i + 1$ *mod* 2.

```
repeat
  flag [i] ← requesting;
  while i ≠ turn ∧ flag [j] ≠ passive do nothing enddo;
  flag [i] ← in-cs;
until flag [j] ≠ in-cs;
turn ← i;
< critical section > ;
turn ← j;
flag [i] ← passive;
```

It is interesting to compare this algorithm with Dekker's. The latter, and all the others, rely on the fairness of the hardware. For example, steps must be taken to ensure that successive conflicts between P_i and P_j for variable *flag* [*i*], where P_i attempts the assignment *flag* [*i*] ← *requesting*, while P_j — which moves very fast and is constantly requesting entry to its critical section — tests for *flag* [*i*] ≠ *passive*, are not always resolved in favour of P_j. If this were the case, P_i would never be able to submit its request, and P_j, never finding *flag* [*i*] ≠ *passive* would access its critical section infinitely often.

With Knuth's algorithm, however, if the processes are in constant conflict for access to their critical section, each in turn will be granted access whatever their respective speeds, which is not the case with Dekker's algorithm. All we know in the latter is that process delay is finite; measuring that delay requires knowledge of the execution speeds.

It is also interesting to see how Knuth's algorithm ensures fair behaviour. The essential difference from Dekker's algorithm is that here the variable *flag* takes three rather than just two values; if *passive* and *false* are semantically the same, in Knuth's algorithm *requesting* and *in-cs* provide more information on the states of the processes than does the Boolean value *true* alone.

2.6. Another fair solution: De Bruijn's algorithm (1967)

De Bruijn (1967) proposed an improvement to Knuth's algorithm, in which the delay function, $d(n)$, is polynomial rather than exponential. All that needs to be done for this optimization is to modify that part of the protocol where *turn* is updated twice, just before and just after the critical section. In De Bruijn's suggestion, the variable is modified only once, as P_i leaves its critical section, provided that its value is the number of the process leaving the critical section (i.e. *turn* = *i*), or that the process whose 'turn' it is is not affected by the mutual exclusion (i.e. *flag turn* = *passive*).

After this slight modification, the protocol for P_i becomes:

```
repeat
    flag [i] ← requesting;
    j ← turn;
    while j ≠ i do
                    if flag [j] ≠ passive then j ← turn
                                         else j ← (j − 1) mod n
                    endif;
          enddo;
    flag [i] ← in-cs;
until testd (i);
< critical section > ;
if flag [turn] = passive turn = i
   then turn ← (turn − 1) mod n
endif;
flag [i] ← passive;
```

PROOF

We shall limit ourselves to demonstrating the fairness of the algorithm and to calculating the corresponding limits. Proofs of mutual exclusion and of critical section reachability are the same as for the previous two algorithms.

The modification made leads to the following observations:

(i) If at a given moment *turn* has the value i and if *flag* $\neq$ *passive*, then *turn* will not change its value until P_i has executed the critical section.

(ii) As long as *turn* keeps the same value, no process can enter its critical section twice. Suppose P_j makes two accesses to its critical section: we will then have *turn* $\neq j$ and *flag* [*turn*] $\neq$ *passive*, for otherwise *turn* would have been modified the first time P_j went through the critical section; furthermore, P_k (for which $k = turn$) has not entered its critical section before P_j, or it would have modified the value of *turn* before P_j passed through for the second time. Consequently *flag* [k] $\neq$ passive, and $k = turn$, during both of P_j's passages through its critical section. It follows that P_j cannot execute its internal loop after it has passed through its critical section once, as these conditions are precisely the loop conditions.

Given these two points, we can conclude that if a process P_i attempts to enter its critical section (i.e. *flag* [i] $\neq$ *passive*), the maximum time for which it is delayed is limited to $d(n) = n(n - 1)$. Before P_i can enter its critical section *turn* can take at most all the $n - 1$ values preceding it in the cyclic order $i - 1$, ..., 0, $n - 1$, ..., $i + 1$, and for each of these values of *turn*, each of the other processes P_j ($j \neq i$) will enter its critical section once at most, so the total delay is $(n - 1)(n - 1)$ turns, to which a further $(n - 1)$ turns may be added when *turn* $= i$, giving $n(n - 1)$ turns in all.

The limit can be reduced still further, as we shall show for process P_0 alone.

(iii) If j takes a value from amongst 1, ..., $n - 1$, then while *flag* [0] $\neq$ *passive* and $j \leqslant turn \leqslant 0$, P_j cannot enter its critical section more than once, because after its first passage through the critical section we cannot have *turn* $= j$; we then have $j > turn \leqslant 0$, which will cause P_j to loop in its second internal loop while *flag* [0] $\neq$ *passive*.

Given points (i), (ii) and (iii), it follows that while *flag* [0] $\neq$ *passive* P_j cannot enter its critical section more than $(n - j)$ times (where each time, $j < turn$, with *turn* taking values cyclically from amongst $n - 1$, $n - 2$, ..., 1, 0, $n - 1$). Process P_0 will then at worst wait a number of turns given by:

$$\sum_{j=1}^{n-1} (n - j) = \frac{n(n - 1)}{2}$$

This limit is the same for all processes, as there is no privileged process and variable *turn* describes a cycle. We leave it to the reader to show that this limit can be reached in practice.

2.7. Further optimization: Eisenberg and MacGuire's algorithm (1972)

Whereas the delay, expressed in numbers of turns as a function of the number of processes, is exponential in Knuth's solution, and quadratic in the optimization given by De Bruijn, Eisenberg and McGuire (1972) proposed a new solution in which the delay is linear. Inspired by Dijkstra's and Knuth's algorithms, it differs essentially in the postlude, which assigns a value to *turn* that allows process delays to be reduced. Note that linear waiting is not FIFO: a process may overtake another no more than once from the moment its request to enter a critical section has been expressed. With the same shared and local variables as before, the protocol for P_i becomes the following:

```
repeat
  flag [i] ← requesting;
  j ← turn;
  while j ≠ i do
              if flag [j] ≠ passive then j ← turn
                                    else j ← (j + 1) mod n
              endif;
          enddo;
  flag [i] ← in-cs;
  j ← 0;
  while (j < n) ∧ (j = i or flag [j] ≠ in-cs)
              do j ← (j + 1) enddo;
until (j ≤ n) ∧ (turn = i ∨ flag [turn] = passive);
turn ← i;
< critical section > ;
j ← (turn + 1) mod n;
while (j ≠ turn) ∧ (flag [j] = passive) do j ← (j + 1) mod n enddo;
turn ← j;
flag [i] ← passive;
```

PROOF

The proof that the algorithm implements mutual exclusion is similar to the one given for Dijkstra's algorithm, the only difference here being the additional constraint on leaving the external loop of the prelude.

To prove that processes will not block each other (critical section reachability) we start by observing that the value of *turn* remains constant. Consequently the first process in the cyclic order *turn, turn* − 1, 1, ..., 0, $n-1$, ..., *turn* + 1 that attempts to enter its critical section will do so without difficulty.

To prove that starvation is avoided, i.e. that there is fairness, we have only to consider the fact that when a process leaves its critical section it explicitly designates the first waiting process, in the cyclic order defined above, as its successor. This also ensures that the time a process remains waiting is limited to $d(n) = n - 1$ turns; this limit is reached by P_i when all processes are attempting to enter the critical section and the variable $turn = i + 1$.

2.8. A didactic approach: Doran and Thomas's algorithms (1980)

Doran and Thomas (1980) give two algorithms that implement a mutual exclusion protocol for two processes P_0 and P_1. These are variants of Dekker's algorithm, drawn up by the authors when they were looking for a simple way of presenting it and making it understandable, for educational purposes.

ALGORITHM 1

Having observed that the two nested loops in Dekker's algorithm did little to make it understandable, Doran and Thomas's first algorithm offers a protocol in which the two loops are encountered sequentially.
With the following shared variables:

    var flag : *array* 0 .. 1 *of boolean*;
      turn : 0 .. 1;

initialized to false and to some arbitrary value respectively, the protocol for P_i is as follows, where i is 0 or 1 and $j = (i + 1)$ *mod* 2:

    flag [*i*] ← *true*;
    if flag [*j*] **then**
      begin
          if *turn* = *j* **then**
                  begin *flag* [*i*] ← *false*;
                      while turn = *j do nothing* **enddo**;
                      flag [*i*] ← *true*;
                end;
        endif;
      end;
    < *critical section* > ;
    turn ← *j*;
    flag [*i*] ← *false*;

This solution is almost trivially derivable from Dekker's algorithm, once the observation has been made that waiting in the internal loop occurs only once; P_i is blocked in that loop when $turn = j$, so once it is released $turn = i$, and since it alone will set $turn$ to value j whatever the value of *flag* [*j*], the test $turn = j$ will be false and the internal loop will not again be executed. Dekker's algorithm and this variant of it essentially follow the same sequence of tests and updating. As the algorithm is the same as Dekker's, it has the same properties — mutual exclusion, avoidance of deadlock.

ALGORITHM 2

The second solution is a development of the first, which replaces the two delays and the variable *flag* by one delay and two state variables. The algorithm is based on the reasoning given above. Consider the following statements from the previous algorithm (which are also in Dekker):

> *flag* $[i] \leftarrow$ *false*;
> **while** *turn* $= j$ **do** *nothing* **enddo**;
> *flag* $[i] \leftarrow$ *true*;

Conceptually, the statements implement a courtesy protocol of the 'after you' type when two processes come into conflict, but the use for this purpose of state variable *flag* $[i]$, which relates to the critical section, makes it difficult to understand. This led to the idea of introducing a supplementary variable for each process P_i — the variable *after-you* $[i]$ — to express this protocol.

The variables shared by P_0 and P_1 then become:

> **var** *flag*: **array** $[0 .. 1]$ **of** *boolean*;
> *after-you* : **array** $[0 .. 1]$ **of** *boolean*;
> *turn* : $0 .. 1$;

Booleans are initialized to false and *turn* to an arbitrary value. The algorithm for P_i becomes the following:

> *flag* $[i] \leftarrow$ *true*;
> **if** *flag* $[j]$ **then**
>   **begin** *after-you* $[i] \leftarrow$ *true*;
>   **while** *flag* $[j]$ $\wedge$
> $(turn = j$ $\vee$ *after-you* $[j] =$ *false*$)$
>   **do** *nothing* **enddo**;
>   *after-you* $[i] \leftarrow$ *false*;
>   **end**;
> $<$ *critical section* $>$;
> *turn* $\leftarrow j$;
> *flag* $[i] \leftarrow$ *false*;

Note that the condition for entry into the critical section is now different from that in algorithm 1 (or in Dekker). When P_i enters its critical section we have:

$$(flag [j] = false) \vee (turn = i \wedge after\text{-}you [j] = true)$$

unlike the previous case, we can therefore have *flag* $[j] =$ *true* when P_i enters its critical section, but this will cause no problems as under those circumstances *after-you* [j] = *true*, which guarantees that P_j is not yet in its critical section.

PROOF OF ALGORITHM 2

Proof that the algorithm operates properly is by contradiction, and case analysis.

Suppose, first of all, that P_i and P_j are both in their critical section. They cannot have entered them simultaneously, because otherwise at the end of their delays in the prelude we would have had:

$$(flag \; [j] = false) \lor (turn = i \land after\text{-}you \; [j] = true)$$
$$\land \; (flag \; [i] = false) \lor (turn = j \land after\text{-}you \; [i] = true)$$

and since at that moment *flag* [k] = *true* $\land$ after-you [k] = *false* (with k = i, j), we should therefore have *turn* = i = j, which is impossible. One of the two, say P_j, must have been the first to enter its critical section. At that moment P_i is in its waiting loop or has not yet entered it, and will not be able to leave it because the wait condition will remain true as long as P_j has not executed the postlude. P_i cannot be between the loop and its critical section, because in that case the condition for it to advance would have been fulfilled at the same time as or before P_j's, which contradicts our starting hypothesis.

Deadlock cannot take place either. If neither process is in its critical section and both are attempting to access it, they can get as far as the loop that causes them to wait. For them to become blocked, the following two conditions must be fulfilled:

$$flag \; [j] \; \land \; (turn = j \lor after\text{-}you \; [j] = false)$$
$$flag \; [i] \; \land \; (turn = i \lor after\text{-}you \; [i] = false)$$

but, as we have seen, we then find that the variables *flag* [k] = *true* and *after-you* [k] = *true*, which means that *turn* = i = j which is impossible. The process indexed by *turn* will therefore find that its condition is false and will thus be able to enter its critical section.

2.9. A simple solution: Peterson's algorithm (1981)

In a paper with a deliberately provocative title, 'Myths about the mutual exclusion problem', Peterson (1981) gave an elegant and very simple solution to this problem. The variables shared between the processes are the same as before – *flag* [i], which is initialized to false, indicates the position of P_i with respect to the mutual exclusion, and *turn* resolves simultaneity conflicts:

```
var flag : array [0 .. 1] of boolean;
    turn : 0 .. 1;
```

The protocol followed by P_i is the following $[i = 0, 1$ and $j = (i + 1)$ *mod* 2)

flag $[i] \leftarrow$ *true* ;
turn $\leftarrow i$;
wait flag $[j] = false \lor turn = j$;
$<$ *critical section* $>$;
flag $[i] \leftarrow$ *false* ;

PROOF

To demonstrate that this algorithm maintains mutual exclusion, suppose that P_0 and P_1 are both in their critical sections. We then have *flag* $[0] = flag$ $[1] = true$. Their tests for entry into the critical section cannot have been true at the same time, as the shared variable *turn* must have been favourable to one process or the other, and the other parts of the conditions must have been false. One of the processes therefore entered its critical section first, say P_i, because it has found *turn* $= j$. P_j could not therefore have entered its critical section with P_i, because it would have needed to find *turn* $= i$, and the only assignment that it could have made to *turn* is unfavourable to itself. Mutual exclusion is therefore maintained.

Mutual blocking of processes is not possible either. Consider P_0 blocked in its wait loop. Within a finite time, P_1 will have no interest in its critical section, will be waiting for it, or will be using its critical section again and again and therefore monopolizing access to it. In the first case *flag* $[1] = false$ and P_0 may enter its critical section. The second case is impossible, as *turn*, which must necessarily be equal to 0 or 1, will make one or other condition true. In the third case, when P_1 attempts to use its critical section again, it will reset *turn* $\leftarrow 1$, which will validate the condition for P_0. This therefore also guarantees fairness.

This algorithm therefore has the same properties as Knuth's, reduced to the special case of two processes: in cases of continual conflict, the critical section will be allocated to each process in turn.

Comment

(a) The variable *flag* only takes two values here, but this behaviour is a consequence of an entirely new approach to the design of the algorithm — readers would do well to compare this solution with those proposed by Knuth and Dekker.

(b) Protocol may be viewed as the 'union' of two simpler protocols that ensure mutual exclusion but do not avoid deadlock; they are obtained by eliminating variables *flag* and *turn* respectively from the text above.

GENERALIZATION TO THE CASE OF n PROCESSES

Having stated that the ostensibly trivial generalization of Dekker's protocol to the case of n processes is, in fact, mythical (it is interesting to compare the very different forms of Dekker's and Dijkstra's protocols), Peterson showed that his solution could easily be generalized. The principle is simple: the solution for the two process case is used repetitively $(n-1)$ times to eliminate at least one process each time, until there is only one left.

The necessary shared variables are:

> *var flag* : *array* $[0 .. n-1]$ *of* $-1 .. n-2$;
> *turn* : *array* $[0 .. n-2]$ *of* $0 .. n-1$;

which are respectively initialized to -1 and 0. There are therefore $2n-1$ variables of size n. The protocol for P_i, with $i = 0$ to $n-1$, uses local variables i and j:

> *for* $j = 0$ *to* $n-2$ *do*
> > *begin*
> > > *flag* $[i] \leftarrow j$;
> > > *turn* $[j] \leftarrow i$;
> > > *wait* $(\forall k \neq i : flag [k] < j) \lor turn [j] \neq i$;
> >
> > *end* ;
>
> $<$ *critical section* $>$;
> *flag* $[i] \leftarrow -1$;

Variable *flag* has been generalized, while -1 plays the same role as *false* did previously, to express the fact that P_i has not entered its critical section. The act of entering a critical section, previously expressed by *true*, is now specified with respect to each of the other processes. In the same way, for variable *turn*, which handles conflicts between pairs of processes, P_i will be delayed to the jth conflict if *turn* $[j] \neq i$. When P_i enters its critical section, we have:

$$\{\forall k \neq i : flag [k] < (n-2)\} \lor (turn [n-2] \neq i)$$

in other words, either P_i has the highest possible value for *flag* $[i] = n-2$, or it is not delayed by the $(n-2)$th and last of all conflicts.

It can easily be seen that the assumption that two processes are in their critical sections leads to a contradiction, and that deadlock is avoided (we have only to generalize the last proof).

This protocol also guarantees fairness. Consider the extreme case in which all processes are attempting to access their critical sections. At the first cycle, since $\forall k \neq i : flag [k] < j$ is false for all processes, only one — P_i, the last to have set *turn* $[0] \leftarrow i$ — is blocked. In the worst possible case, it was the first to arrive and will then be overtaken by the other $(n-1)$ processes.

Assuming the least favourable conditions, these $(n-1)$ processes will each request mutual exclusion, but at that point P_i will necessarily be unblocked and it will be P_1, the last to have assigned a value to variable *turn* $[0]$, that will be blocked instead. We are then left with an $(n-1)$ process situation. If, therefore, $d(n)$ is the number of turns a process may be required to wait, when there are n processes:

$$d(n) = n - 1 + d(n - 1)$$

which gives: $d(n) = n(n-1)/2$ turns. This protocol therefore has the same limit as De Bruijn's protocol; note that the limit may be reached by both.

2.10. Minimizing the number of values used: Burns' algorithm (1981)

When he turned his attention to the problem of mutual exclusion, Burns (1981) set out to find solutions that were symmetrical (i.e. the same for all processes), and that used a minimum number of variables, and a minimum number of values taken by these variables.

He proved several theorems concerning various definitions of symmetry. For example, the strictest symmetry constraint that we can adopt to solve the mutual exclusion problem is weak symmetry: in its initial state a process cannot be distinguished from any of the other processes. He proved that on this assumption any protocol, based on read and write primitives, which solves mutual exclusion and avoids deadlock, must use at least $n + 1$ variables, n of size 2 (Booleans), and one whose size must be at least n.

By way of illustration of these results, Burns proposed a protocol that improves on Dijkstra's — which, it should be remembered, uses n three-valued variables and one shared variable taking any of n distinct values. The variables shared by processes P_0, ..., P_i, ..., P_{n-1} are

> *var flag* : *array* [0 .. $n - 1$] *of boolean* ;
> *turn* : 0 .. $n - 1$;

The protocol for process P_i is as follows (we have reformulated it in such a way as to eliminate branching statements; variable j is local):

```
flag [i]  ←  true;
turn  ←  i;
repeat
while turn ≠ i do
        begin
        flag [i]  ←  false;
        j ← 1;
        while (j < n) ∧ (j = i ∨ flag [j] = false)
        do j ← j + 1 enddo;
        if j ⩾ n then
                begin
                flag [i]  ←  true;
                turn  ←  i;
        end;
```

```
        endif ;
    end ;
        j ← 1;
        while (j < n) ∧ (j = i ∨ flag [j] = false)
                        do j ← j + 1 enddo ;
until j ⩾ n ;
< critical section > ;
flag [i] ← false ;
```

PROOF

We prove the mutual exclusion property by contradiction. If P_i and P_j are simultaneously in their critical sections, each of them will have found the other's *flag* variable set to false, which is impossible: before entering its critical section, a process P_k must find *turn* = k, but it is the only process that will carry out the statement *turn* ← k, which must always be preceded by *flag* [k] ← *true*.

Similar reasoning will show that deadlock is avoided. Let P_i be the process that last carried out the assignment *turn*(←)i. Consequently all the other blocked processes P_k will find *flag* [i] = *true* and will therefore loop through **while turn ≠ i do ... enddo**, setting their variable *flag* [k] ← *false*, with the consequence that P_i will be able to enter its critical section. To complete the proof, we must also show that if deadlock takes place, there is a process P_i that will be the last to have assigned *turn* ← i, after which assignment *turn* is not modified again. For this to happen, another process must have made the assignment *turn* ← j, but then P_j would have found *flag* [i] = *false* : ∀ i ≠ j. This is either true, in which case P_j may enter its critical section, or it is false, which leads to a contradiction.

Comment

Burns and Lynch (1980) showed that a mutual exclusion protocol avoiding deadlock (leaving symmetry considerations to one side) must use at least n binary shared variables.

Chapter 3

The mutual exclusion problem in a centralized framework: hardware solutions

This chapter discusses some specialized instructions which are implemented or may be implemented on many machines.

After a brief discussion of solutions to the problem on uniprocessor machines, we shall consider statements designed for multiprocessors. We shall conclude the chapter with a few comments on the semaphore concept.

3.1. Uniprocessor machines

A uniprocessor machine may have parallel processing aspects, but only in its input/output devices: a process may be delayed by an interrupt issued by a peripheral caused by another process executing an input/output instruction. So even though there is only one CPU, it cannot guarantee that the critical section of a particular process will be executed: actions for which the critical code in a process is responsible, and those depending on the interrupt, may overlap in actual execution.

To avoid this, and therefore to be able to implement critical sections in which the presence of one process will exclude that of all the others, all we need is to be able to guarantee that there is some sequence of actions that is indivisible. As the only possible interference in the execution of a process arises from interrupts, we have to be able to inhibit such interrupts, which we shall call masked interrupts. Inhibition in this way may be implemented by primitives defined by the system kernel, which implements the mutual exclusion protocol in the same way for every process, as follows:

```
< code >;
mask ;
< critical section >;
unmask ;
< code >;
```

Only the < code > parts can then be interrupted, while the < critical section > part cannot.

With this elementary mechanism at our disposal, we can build up others that are more sophisticated (Zelkowitz 1971) to meet the needs of particular applications [conditional wait, queue management, etc. — see Shaw (1974), Crocus (1975), Haberman (1976), Peterson and Silberschatz (1983)].

Comment

A trivial solution to the problem would be to guarantee indivisibility by preventing the CPU being shared between different processes. A process requesting an input/output operation will not release the CPU and simply waits (i.e. remains in occupation of the CPU) until the end of the input/output operation. It is informed of completion of the input/output operation by an interrupt, after which it continues execution. Such a solution, although it eliminates the need for the primitives discussed above, is unacceptable: performance levels rapidly fall off owing to the slowness of peripheral devices, particularly in view of what can be done if several input/output operations are executed simultaneously under genuinely parallel conditions.

In summary, for a uniprocessor the mutual exclusion problem can be solved by defining the interrupt mask and unmask primitives.

3.2. Multiprocessor machines

In cases where several processors may access a common memory, the fundamental mechanism provided by the hardware is mutual exclusion to any single memory location. Even if we consider a uniprocessor and its input/output devices as several processors, the problems posed by a multiprocessor are fundamentally different. In the first case, the relations of a uniprocessor to its input/output processors, which use interrupts to inform it of the end of a service that they have provided, are marked by asymmetric behaviour of the 'master-slave' type. In the multiprocessor case, on the other hand, all the processors behave in a way that can be assumed to be identical: their behaviour is 'egalitarian'. There is no interrupt mechanism between processors on which mutual exclusion could be based (interrupt masking is, of course, still a possible way of implementing mutual exclusion between processors and their input/output devices — see Carver Hill 1973).

The need for specialized instructions has led machine designers to propose several possibilities. The common factor linking all these instructions and distinguishing them from all others, is the fact that they carry out two actions atomically: e.g. reading and writing, or reading and testing, of a single memory location within one instruction fetch cycle.

It should be remembered that, in any machine, access to a memory location excludes any other access to the same word. It is on the basis of this fundamental exclusion that algorithms and instructions for exclusion in a centralized system are constructed.

3.2.1. Exchange instruction

Instruction *exchange* (*r,m*) will exchange the contents of register *r* with those of memory location *m*. During execution of this instruction access to *m* is blocked for any other instruction using *m*.

The mutual exclusion protocol uses a variable shared by all processes: memory location *bolt* initialized to 1; it may take values 0 or 1. Each process P_i uses a local variable *key* (a processor register), which also only takes values 0 or 1. The protocol for process P_i is then as follows, with *bolt* and *key* initialized to 1 and 0 respectively:

> *repeat exchange* (*key$_i$*, *bolt*)
> *until key* = 1;
> < *critical section* >;
> *exchange* (*key$_i$*, *bolt*);

A process will only be allowed to enter its critical section if it finds *bolt* set to 1. It will then exclude all other processes from the critical section by setting *bolt* to 0. It releases the critical section by setting *bolt* to 1, thereby allowing a waiting process to enter the critical section. If two processes arrive simultaneously, their execution of *exchange* will be sequentialized, i.e. one will come after the other in some arbitrary order, because of the nature of the memory access mechanism, which allows only one access at a time to word *bolt*.

Note that only process P_i in its critical section satisfies $key_i = 1$, and that the following relation on variables *key* and *bolt* is true at all times (initially, and before or after every call to *exchange*):

$$\sum_i key_i + bolt = 1$$

which is the invariant for this solution to the problem — it ensures, given the range of values (covering integers 0 and 1), that not more than one process is in its critical section, while if *bolt* equals 1, no process is in its critical section.

3.2.2. Test and set instruction

The instruction *testset* (*m*) carries out a series of actions atomically: it tests the value of variable *m*; if the value is 0, it replaces it by 1 and gives the result *true*; otherwise, it makes no change to the value of *m* and returns *false* as a result. Alternatively, this instruction could be considered as acting on the machine's program counter rather than giving a Boolean result (Crocus 1975).

The mutual exclusion protocol implemented using this instruction requires a shared variable *bolt* initialized to 0. The protocol is as follows for each process P_i:

> *repeat nothing*
> *until testset* (*bolt*);
> < *critical section* >;
> *bolt* ← 0;

The only process that can be in its critical section is the one that found *bolt* set to 0. Once a process P_i is in its critical section, all those processes wishing to enter their own critical section are delayed, in the active mode, in their entry protocol. As soon as P_i has executed its exit protocol, one and only one of the waiting processes will be able to enter its critical section.

Burns et al. (1982) analyses the shared memory needs associated with mutual exclusion between *n* processes under conditions guaranteeing fairness while avoiding deadlock, using such a *testset* primitive. Upper and lower limits for the number of values needed are given for each of the problems studied.

3.2.3. Lock instruction

The definition of this instruction is very similar to that of *testset*. Here, however, the wait loop is an integral part of the instruction itself, whereas before it was external to it.

The behaviour of atomic lock and unlock instructions is best described by the following algorithms (Shaw 1974):

> *lock* (*m*) ≡ **begin**
>   **repeat** *nothing* **while** $m = 1$;
> $m \leftarrow 1$;
>   **end** ;
>   *unlock* (*m*) ≡ $m \leftarrow 0$

Given a shared variable *bolt* initialized to 0, the mutual exclusion protocol takes the following form:

> *lock* (*bolt*);
> < *critical section* >;
> *unlock* (*bolt*);

In some machines the lock instruction is called TSB (Test and Switch Branch). It is sufficient to provide a critical section entry protocol, with a *bolt* variable initialized to an appropriate value.

3.2.4. Increment instruction

The effect of increment and decrement instructions, which we shall call *addc* (*r*,*m*) and *subc* (*r*,*m*) (see Haberman 1976), is to increment or decrement, respectively, the content of memory location *m* by 1 and to load the result into register *r*.

Using the same notation as before, the exclusion protocol for process P_i can be implemented using the *subc* instruction alone. *Bolt* is initialized to 1.

> **repeat** *subc* (*key*, *bolt*)
>   **until** $key = 0$;
> < *critical section* >;
> *bolt* $\leftarrow 1$;

Shown graphically, the history of variable *bolt* would appear as follows:

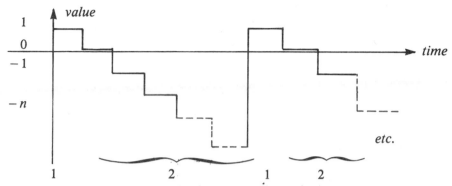

Where: 1, one process obtains mutually exclusive access
                2, one or more processes awaiting entry to the critical section.

Mutual exclusion can be implemented in an entirely analogous way using instruction *addc* (*key, bolt*), but with variable *bolt* initialized to -1.

In practice, the use of either of these instructions on machines implementing them would have one major disadvantage: if a process remains in possession of the critical section for a long time while several others are trying to access it, variable *bolt* will grow — or decrease — indefinitely. Depending on the size of the memory location, this could lead to major problems causing the procedure to fail, either because an overflow takes place causing memory failure or because the variable returns to value 1, as a result of growth modulation of the word size.

3.2.5. Replace-add instruction

Instruction *repadd* was proposed for computers whose addressing system uses an interconnection network (Gottlieb et al. 1983). Instruction *repadd* (m,v) atomically adds the contents of m and value v, stores the sum in m and returns it as a result.

A mutual exclusion protocol can be implemented using variable *bolt* shared by all the processes and initialized to 1. Variables ok_i are local to processes P_i.

```
oki ← false;
repeat if bolt − 1 ⩾ 0 then
      if repadd (bolt, − 1) ⩾ 0
          then oki ← true
          else repadd (bolt, 1);
      endif;
  endif;
until oki;
< critical section >;
repadd (bolt, 1);
```

The tests carried out in the second and third lines of the entry protocol may seem redundant, but this is far from the case. They are there to make the solution independent of process execution speed. Suppose for a moment that we discarded the test carried out in the second line, and consider what would happen if two processes are waiting in a loop for entry to their critical section, while a third is about to execute its exit protocol. The value of *bolt* will then be -2. When the third process exits, *bolt* will return to -1. It would then be possible for both waiting processes to dovetail their actions in such a way that *bolt* would take values 0 and -1 without ever reaching the value 1 needed to allow access to the critical section, with the result that the critical section would be no longer reachable. The test provided in line 2 avoids this problem.

Such an instruction is particularly valuable if the machine uses an Ω interconnection network as its addressing mechanism. Conflicts over access to memory between read, write and *repadd* instructions are handled at each stage of the network, and the time taken for each instruction is independent of whether or not conflict takes place (memory modules and elementary switches on the network are equipped with adders).

3.3. Overview of the semaphore concept

3.3.1. General

The solutions to the mutual exclusion problem discussed above all have certain disadvantages. First, there is the active wait problem: a process that is doing nothing none the less occupies the processor, which limits the efficiency of the system kernel and therefore leads to loss of performance. Secondly, there is the difficulty of generalizing these solutions to more complex problems. These considerations led Dijkstra to define the semaphore concept (Dijkstra 1965). Although few machines have introduced the semaphore concept into their instruction set, we shall none the less deal with it in this chapter on hardware implementations, because it is a machine level primitive and not a language construct intended to express control. It was therefore an entirely deliberate choice of ours to treat it as belonging to the same level as branching and sequential control instructions: these are all target instructions of the structured statements of high-level languages. Semaphores and their primitives, whether hard wired or implemented using statements of the *testset* type, are therefore generally offered as fundamental tools of system kernels.

A semaphore s is a non-negative integer variable that can be handled only by the following two primitives:

$P(s)$: **if** $s \leqslant 0$ **then** *wait in a queue associated with s* **endif**;
$\quad\quad\quad s \leftarrow s - 1$;
$V(s)$: $s \leftarrow s + 1$;
$\quad\quad\quad$ **if** $s \leqslant 0$ **then** *unblock one of the waiting processes* **endif**;

By definition only a single primitive may be executed on any one semaphore at any one time. As may be seen, a queue is associated with every semaphore and contains all the processes blocked at that semaphore. Initially, the semaphore must have a non-negative integer value, and its associated queue is empty. The mutual exclusion protocol can be coded as follows, using a semaphore *mutex* initialized to 1:

> $P(mutex)$;
> $<$ *critical section* $>$;
> $V(mutex)$;

It is clearly very simple to use primitives associated with the semaphore concept. If *mutex* is initialized to value v, up to v processes will be allowed to enter the controlled section. Mutual exclusion then becomes a particular case of a more general problem: how can we prevent the number of processes simultaneously using a section of code rising above a predefined limit?

Consequently semaphores are tools making it possible to resolve various other control problems, e.g. process coordination problems, which makes the concept extremely valuable. Proof mechanisms associated with semaphores have been proposed by Haberman (1972), and interested readers will find detailed studies on the semaphore concept in Dijkstra (1968, 1971), Patil (1971), Kosaraju (1973), and Presser (1975). More particularly, Crocus (1975) and Peterson and Silberschatz (1983) discuss implementation techniques and Stark (1982) gives formal definitions of the various semaphores to be found in the literature on the subject and a critical study of their relative advantages and disadvantages.

Furthermore, Brinch Hansen (1972) discusses the critical region and conditional critical region ideas, which can be viewed as methodologies for using the semaphore concept. Again, Schmidt (1976) gives a detailed study on systematic and efficient determination of triggering conditions associated with critical regions. Finally, the monitor notion was introduced simultaneously by Brinch Hansen (1973) and Hoare (1974) on the basis of the 'secretary' concept originally advanced by Dijkstra (1971). It provides a synchronization tool found in many languages and may consequently be viewed as a parallelism control mechanism for a particularly sophisticated abstract machine, offered by certain system kernels to their users (see Lister and Maynard 1976 or Kessels 1977).

3.3.2. Morris's algorithm

If several processes are blocked on semaphore s, two possibilities exist for what will happen when $V(s)$ operates, depending on whether we treat the structure within which the processes are blocked as a set or a FIFO queue. Definitions associated with each of these possibilities are to be found in Dijkstra (1965) or Haberman (1972), and Dijkstra (1971). They are generally qualified as *weak* and *strong* definitions of semaphores.

In the case of the strong definition — for which the waiting structure is a FIFO file — the definition of primitives cannot lead to a starvation problem, as blocked processes are reactivated in the order in which they were suspended. Any starvation that may occur must therefore be due to their being badly used in the algorithm in which they appear.

The same is not true if the waiting structure is a set, i.e. in the case of the weak semaphore definition. If there are always some processes waiting at semaphore s, there is no guarantee that a process will not remain indefinitely blocked at s, as processes reactivated by $V(s)$ operations are chosen 'randomly' from amongst the set of blocked processes.

In 1978 Dijkstra put forward the conjecture that there was no solution to the mutual exclusion problem avoiding starvation, applicable to an unknown but finite number of processes, using a finite number of weak semaphores.

Morris (1979), however, refuted this conjecture, by proposing an algorithm that solves the posed problem. This solution uses three semaphores with the following behaviour: if one or several processes are waiting in a $P(s)$ operation and another process is executing $V(s)$, the value of semaphore s is not modified and one of the waiting processes is unblocked independently of $P(s)$.

Apart from the three semaphores, the algorithm uses two non-negative integer variables as counters of the number of processes in certain sections:

> **var** a, b, m : **semaphore**;
> na, nm : $0 .. + \infty$;

Semaphores a and b are initialized to 1, while semaphore m and counters na and nm are initialized to 0.

We shall start by stating the algorithm and then give an informal explanation of it. A formal demonstration of its properties based on axiomatic techniques is given in Morris (1979). The protocol is the same for all processes.

> $P(b)$; $na \leftarrow na + 1$; $V(b)$;
> $P(a)$; $nm \leftarrow nm + 1$;
> $P(b)$; $na \leftarrow na - 1$;
>   **if** $na = 0$ **then** $V(b)$; $V(m)$
>   **else** $V(b)$; $V(a)$
>   **endif**;
> $P(m)$; $nm \leftarrow nm - 1$;
> $<$ *critical section* $>$;
> **if** $nm = 0$ **then** $V(a)$
>   **else** $V(m)$
> **endif**;

As a study of the topology of the protocol will show, the mutual exclusion semaphore b protects access to the shared variable na. A process attempting to enter its critical section must cross two 'barriers' represented by semaphores a and m. Counters na and nm respectively contain the number of processes ready to cross barrier a, and those having already crossed barrier a but not yet barrier m. Note that a process having crossed $P(a)$ while there are still several processes waiting for $P(a)$ will find that $na > 0$ and will execute $V(a)$, thereby releasing these processes. The processes will then be blocked on $P(m)$, which is initialized to zero. Once the last process blocked on $P(a)$ has been released, it will find $na = 0$, and will open the m barrier, allowing a process to cross $P(m)$. Barrier a is then closed [there has been one more $P(a)$ executed than $V(a)$], and a is initialized to 1. Note too that any P-operation on a or m is followed by a V-operation on a or m and that the initial value of $a + m$ is 1, so we have the invariant $0 \leqslant a + m \leqslant 1$.

This leads to the start of the second part of the protocol: the nm processes blocked at $P(m)$ will enter their critical sections one by one, using a 'cascade' technique similar to that used in the first phase. Once the last of the nm processes has executed its exit protocol, it will open a by means of $V(a)$, and the cycle can start again.

This informal description of the algorithm shows how it was developed. A formal treatment and proof that it has the properties expected of it (mutual exclusion, avoidance of deadlock, avoidance of starvation) are given by the author (Morris 1979). They are based on the axiomatic reasoning developed by Gries and Owicki for the predicate aspects (mutual exclusion and avoidance of deadlock), and on dynamic behaviour analysis (which axiomatic reasoning cannot take into account) for their starvation avoidance.

This algorithm also has another major advantage, in that it demolishes what is today a very widespread myth concerning the use of semaphores, according to which inverting two consecutive V-operations will not prevent the program being correct. This is totally false. Inverting $V(a)$ and $V(b)$ in the first *if ... endif* conditional construction in the algorithm will deprive it of its starvation avoidance property. It is easy to construct a counter example using three processes Q_0, Q_1, and Q_2. We shall distinguish the two executions of $P(b)$ in the algorithm using the notation $P^1(b)$ and $P^2(b)$. Q_0 is blocked on $P^1(b)$, Q_1 is blocked on $P(a)$ and Q_2 is about to execute $V(a)$; $V(b)$. Once Q_2 has executed $V(a)$, Q_1 will move rapidly forward and find itself blocked on $P^2(b)$. If, now, the execution of $V(b)$ by Q_2 releases Q_1, the latter will find $na = 0$ and will open barrier m to process Q_2, which can then overtake process Q_0 in $P^1(b)$, by requesting the exclusion once more.

Chapter 4

The mutual exclusion problem in a distributed framework: solutions based on state variables

4.1. Introduction

If we are to speak meaningfully of distributed algorithms we shall need to define carefully what we understand by the word 'distributed'. We shall use the term for two types of algorithm that are distinguished by the way in which they are expressed and by the mechanisms corresponding to those forms of expression. What they have in common is their independence of any centralized entity, such as a memory location or a clock.

One form of expression is based on the communication of messages to carry the necessary information between processes provided with local memories which are inaccessible to other processes. Algorithms based on this approach are of considerable value in networks, whatever their technology or topology. The suitability of such algorithms to structures of this kind is obvious, given the specific characteristics of this form of expression. Such algorithms will be studied in Chapter 5.

In this chapter we shall be concerned with the other kind of distributed algorithm. These are based on the use of state variables, but here, unlike with centralized algorithms, we shall no longer be using global variables such as *turn*, which any process could access for reading or writing. The only permitted variables will be those of local or specific type, using the terms with the meanings defined in Chapter 2. A variable is *local* to a process if it is inaccessible to other processes, and a variable is *specific* to a process if that process alone may read and write it while other processes may only read it. Distributed algorithms using this form of expression allow processes to obtain information concerning the state of other processes, but on no account to influence that state directly: every process is autonomous, and there is no centralized device for resolving conflicts.

The value of this 'pseudo-centralized' form based on the use of state variables is the ease and clarity that it gives to the definition of algorithms. It is an approach that could be applied in a distributed architecture that uses a communications system based on the exchange of messages. The reading of variables specific to other processes by process P_i would then be represented by two actions: the transmission of a message requesting the value of the variable, followed by the receipt of the message containing the value. Provision would have to be made in the processes containing the variables to be read, for appropriate action to be taken on receipt of an enquiry message. It is then obvious that if the algorithm is expressed directly in architectural terms, two levels would be mixed, the logic of the algorithm and its implementation, making it difficult to describe and understand. Another disadvantage of such an approach is the large number of messages needed when the algorithms are executed. No provision is made for values concerning process states to be transmitted each time states change — as happens in the cases we will consider in the next chapter, where distributed algorithms are based on message communication — but state values are requested independently of whether or not the state has changed; we can say that conceptually this corresponds to 'blind' testing of a state variable, an analogous process to active waiting in the case of centralized algorithms. This can therefore lead to large numbers of unnecessary messages being exchanged between processes if their states have not changed.

It would therefore appear that distributed algorithms based on the use of state variables should be implemented on centralized architectures if they are to be efficient. Under these conditions, they have a major advantage over centralized algorithms, as they depend on no global variables: they tend to be far more fault tolerant — a breakdown in one process will not affect the overall behaviour of the algorithm.

4.2. The bakery algorithm: Lamport (1974)

The first algorithm independent of any centralized device was proposed by Lamport (1974). It applies a very simple operating principle, based on the practice in certain shops in which every customer receives a numbered ticket on arrival, allowing each to be served in turn. Here, since we are avoiding dependence on any centralized device, each of the n processes P_0, ..., P_{n-1} chooses its own number, taking account of the numbers selected by the other processes, and if two processes have chosen the same number we arbitrarily decide that the process with lower index is served first.

The necessary variables are as follows:
  var choice : *array* $[0 .. n-1]$ *of boolean*;
    number : *array* $[0 .. n-1]$ *of integer*;

which are initialized to false and 0 respectively. Note that the pair (*choice* $[i]$, *number* $[i]$) belongs to P_i: P_i may read and write these variables, while P_j ($\forall\, j \neq i$) may only read them.

We shall use the following notation: $<$ is an ordering relation on pairs of integers defined as follows:

$$[(a,\, b) < (c,\, d)] \overset{\triangle}{=} [a < c \vee (a = c \wedge b < d)]$$

The protocol followed by process P_i is as follows, where variable j is local to P_i:

$$choice \; [i] \leftarrow true;$$
$$number \; [i] \leftarrow 1 + max \; (number \; [0] + \; ... \; + number \; [n-1]);$$
$$choice \; [i] \leftarrow false;$$
$$\textbf{for } j = 0 \textbf{ to } n - 1, \; i \neq j$$
$$\textbf{begin}$$
$$\textbf{wait } \neg \; choice \; [j];$$
$$\textbf{wait } (number \; [j] \neq 0) \Rightarrow (number \; [i], i) < (number \; [j], j);$$
$$\textbf{end};$$
$$< critical \; section >;$$
$$number \; [i] \leftarrow 0;$$

PROOF

We shall say that P_i is *entering* when *choice* $[i] = true$, and that it is *inside* between statements *choice* $[i] \leftarrow false$ and *number* $[i] \leftarrow 0$.

It is easy to show that this protocol avoids deadlock and that it guarantees fairness. If processes P_i and P_k are *inside* and P_i was *inside* before P_k became *entering* then *number* $[i] <$ *number* $[k]$. In fact, *number* $[i]$ contains its final value when P_k is calculating *number* $[k]$; we therefore have *number* $[k] \geqslant 1 +$ *number* $[i]$. P_i will therefore enter its critical section before P_k.

This is therefore some kind of FIFO protocol, as any process attempting to enter its critical section will first execute the *entering* part that contains no loop, and will enter its critical section before any process that executes its *entering* part later. If the execution of their *entering* sections coincides in time, the processes will be ordered by the value of their *number* variables, independently of the order in which they arrived at their *entering* section. This protocol therefore ensures that waiting is limited, with a limit given by $d(n) = n - 1$.

To demonstrate mutual exclusion, we prove the following lemma: if P_i is in its critical section and P_k is *inside* — which means that it has calculated *number* $[k]$; then (*number* $[i], i) < ($*number* $[k], k)$. P_k cannot therefore enter its critical section, as it will find *number* $[i] \neq 0 \Rightarrow ($*number* $[k], k) < ($*number* $[i], i)$ false.

To prove the lemma, we shall adopt P_i's point of view and define various times:

. tw_1 : P_i reads *choice* $[k]$ for the last time, for $j = k$, in its first wait, so at tw_1 we have *choice* $[k] = false$.

. tw_2 : P_i begins its final execution, for $j = k$, of the second wait. We therefore have $tw_1 < tw_2$.

. tk_1 : P_k enters its entering zone to calculate *number* $[k]$.

. tk_2 : P_k has finished calculating *number* $[k]$.

. tk_3 : P_k exits the *entering* zone. We have $tk_1 < tk_2 < tk_3$.

Since at tw_1, *choice* $[k] = false$, we have either $tw_1 < tk_1$ or $tk_3 < tw_1$. In the first case, as is clear from the start of our proof of deadlock avoidance, we have *number* $[i] <$ *number* $[k]$, which proves the lemma.

In the second case, we have $tk_2 < tk_3 < tw_1 < tw_2$, which implies $tk_2 < tw_2$. This means that at tw_2, P_i has read the current value of *number* $[k]$. Moreover, as tw_2 is the moment at which the final execution of the second wait for $j = k$ takes place, we have (*number* $[i]$, i) < (*number* $[k]$, k), which completes the proof of the lemma.

It is equally easy to prove that if there is a finite number of process breakdowns, the preceding properties are conserved, as the values of private variables of a broken-down process are set to indicate that it is outside its critical section and its access protocol. If P_i can break down an infinite number of times, the system could block if P_i constantly breaks down as it enters its protocol. Then the other processes, by an unfortunate concatenation of circumstances, would always find *choice* $[i]$ = *true*, and therefore would loop indefinitely.

Comment

A disadvantage of this algorithm is that the values of *number* $[i]$ could increase indefinitely. There is no limit to their growth if there is always at least one process in the *inside* zone. If processes enter the *entering* zone at a maximum rate of 1/ms, then at the end of a year's operations number $[i]$ is close to 2^{35}. This aspect of the distributed algorithm has been improved on since, as will be seen in the following algorithms.

4.3. Dijkstra's self-stabilizing algorithm (1974)

Dijkstra (1974) suggests a distributed mutual exclusion algorithm that has the powerful property of being self-stabilizing. We shall see how it has been improved to make it also more fault-tolerant.

In contrast to the last algorithm, where any process could obtain information about any other, here processes P_0, ..., P_{n-1} have a simple topological structure: they are distributed around a ring (which is, of course, a purely logical structure, entirely independent of physical architecture) around which each process P_i can only request information from its right-hand neighbour P_{i-1} ($i - 1 \bmod n$). For P_i, the privileged state of being in its critical section is then expressed by a configuration involving its own state variable and that of its left-hand neighbour.

The necessary variables for this protocol, with ($k > 1$) are:

var *flag* : **array** $[0 .. n - 1]$ **of** $0 .. k$;

The only actions that P_i may undertake are therefore reading and updating its own variable *flag* $[i]$ and reading *flag* $[i - 1]$. It cannot access any of the other variables.

The protocol proposed is not symmetrical for all processes, as P_0 has a particular role to play.

Protocol for P_0	Protocol for P_i $(i \neq 0)$
wait flag $[0] = flag$ $[n - 1]$;	*wait flag* $[i] \neq flag$ $[i - 1]$; *lag*
< *critical section* >;	< *critical section* >;
flag $[0] \leftarrow (flag$ $[0] + 1)$	*flag* $[i] \leftarrow flag$ $[i - 1]$;
mod k;	

CHARACTERISTICS

This protocol guarantees mutual exclusion, with array *flag* initialized to 0, avoidance of deadlock and fairness. Privilege, i.e. the configuration of state variables allowing entrance to the critical section, moves round the ring of processes which therefore receive it in succession.

The disadvantage of this algorithm is that it forces a process to receive privilege even if it is not attempting to enter its critical section. It must then execute the exit section of its protocol in order to 'transmit' privilege to its left-hand neighbour.

This algorithm has a remarkable property in that it is self-stabilizing if $k > n$. Whatever the values to which variables *flag* $[i]$ are initialized, after a finite number of system transitions we reach a state in which only one process will have privilege. (This is proved in Mossiere et al. 1977.)

Kruijer (1979) gives another algorithm with the same self-stabilization property, but with processes distributed on a tree rather than on a ring.

AN ALGORITHM FOR PROCESSES WITH FOUR STATES

From the control point of view, the algorithm above uses processes that can take k states. Dijkstra proposes two other algorithms, with the self-stabilization property, for processes with three or four states. (It should be remembered that the self-stabilization property in the above algorithm applied only when $k > n$.) We shall only describe the algorithm for processes with four states; it can also be helpful for cases where $n > 4$.

Every process P_i has two binary variables, representing the four states:

> var *flag* $[i]$: *boolean*;
> *direction* $[i]$: (*up, down*);

The algorithm will not need to stabilize itself if the variables are initialized as follows:

> *flag* $[i] = false$, $\forall$ i
> *direction* $[i] = up$, $\forall$ $i \neq 0$
> *direction* $[0] = down$

Direction $[0]$ and *direction* $[n-1]$ remain constant — the processes at the 'ends of the ring' therefore only have two states.

The protocols are as follows:

> for P_0 : PROT'$_2$ *wait flag* $[0] = flag$ $[1] \wedge direction$ $[1] = up$;
> $<$ *critical section* $>$;
>   *flag* $[0] \leftarrow \urcorner$ *flag* $[0]$;

For P_i, the protocol to follow will alternate between PROT$_1$ and PROT$_2$: the first time it accesses the critical section it will use PROT$_1$, the second time PROT$_2$, etc.

> PROT$_1$ *wait flag* $[i] \neq flag$ $[i-1]$;
> $<$ *critical section* $>$;
>   *flag* $[i] \leftarrow flag$ $[i-1]$;
>   *direction* $[i] \leftarrow down$;
>
> PROT$_2$ *wait flag* $[i] = flag$ $[i+1]$;
> $\wedge$ *direction* $[i] = down \wedge direction$ $[i+1] = up$;
> $<$ *critical section* $>$;
>   *direction* $[i] \leftarrow up$;

The protocol for the last process, P_{n-1} is:

> PROT'$_1$ *wait flag* $[i] \neq flag$ $[i-1]$;
> $<$ *critical section* $>$;
>   *flag* $[i] \leftarrow flag$ $[i-1]$;

The lack of symmetry here is even greater than in the last algorithm, as both 'end of ring' processes have different protocols from the other P_i.

We see at once that privilege no longer moves around the ring in a cyclical way from P_0 to P_{n-1} and on to P_0 again, but shuttles backwards and forwards between P_0 and P_{n-1}. If we record both the movement of the privilege and the protocol allowing it to be obtained, we get the following pattern:

> processes P_0 P_1 ... P_{n-2} P_{n-1} P_{n-2} ... P_1 P_0 ...
>
> protocols PROT'$_2$ PROT$_1$ ... PROT$_1$ PROT'$_1$ PROT$_2$ ... PROT$_2$
> PROT'$_2$...

The direction of movement is given within the protocols by values *up* and *down*. PROT$_1$ takes the privileged status upwards from P_0 to P_{n-1}, while PROT$_2$ brings it back down again.

We shall not discuss the three-state algorithm that behaves in an analogous way.

FAULT TOLERANCE

If a process breaks down, it must be eliminated from the virtual ring, which means that the neighbourhood relationship must be redefined (see Mossiere et al. 1977). To make this possible, each process P_i is provided with two further state variables giving information about its neighbours to the left and to the right respectively:

var neighbour : *array* [(*left, right*), 0 .. $n - 1$] *of* 0 .. $n - 1$;

with the initial ring configuration being:
neighbour   [*left, i*] = $i - 1$ *mod n*;
neighbour   [*right, i*] = $i + 1$ *mod n*;

and in the protocol given above we replace $(i - 1)$ by *neighbour* [*left, i*]. Given the asymmetrical nature of the protocol, there are two possible cases if a process disappears from the ring.

If P_i ($i \neq 0$) disappears, there is no problem: we have only to redefine neighbourhood relations. It is up to the communication system to detect P_i's breakdown and to carry out the corresponding P_i disappearance protocol:

neighbour (*right, neighbour* [*left, i*]) $\leftarrow$ *neighbour* [*right, i*];
neighbour (*left, neighbour* [*right, i*]) $\leftarrow$ *neighbour* [*left, i*];

If P_0 disappears, the protocol loses its asymmetric character — incrementation modulo k — and privilege is lost and, although mutual exclusion is preserved, all processes will be blocked. To avoid this possibility we have to find another process to play the role of P_0. The process chosen will be the one with lowest index value. Every process therefore has a protocol that, depending on the value of its index, will make it play the P_0 role or a standard role. The protocol for P_i ($\forall_i$) then becomes the following, which works even if there is only one process:

if neighbour [*left, i*] $\geqslant i$
       then begin
              wait flag [*i*] = *flag* (*neighbour* [*left, i*]);
              < *critical section* >;
              flag [*i*] $\leftarrow$ (*flag* + 1) *mod k*;
       end
else begin

> *wait flag* $[i] \neq flag$ (*neighbour* $[left, i]$);
> $<$ *critical section* $>$;
> *flag* $[i] \leftarrow flag$ (*neighbour* $[left, i]$);
> *end*;
> *endif*;

A process P_i may be reinserted into the ring: it has only to reinitialize its variable *flag* $[i]$ as follows. Since its variables *neighbour* $[right, i]$ and *neighbour* $[left, i]$ will have been updated by the communications system, P_i must follow the following re-entry protocol:

> *if neighbour* $[right, i] < i$
>   *then flag* $[i] \leftarrow flag$ (*neighbour* $[right, i-1]$) *mod k*
> *else flag* $[i] \leftarrow$ (*neighbour* $[right, i]$)
> *endif*;

P_i's right-hand neighbour must not communicate the value of its *flag* variable when asked to do so if at that moment it holds privilege, otherwise two processes would have privilege at the same time.

Comment

In implementations on a distributed architecture, this protocol requires that the three variables *flag* $[i]$, neighbour $[right, i]$ and *neighbour* $[left, i]$ should be placed on site P_i. Reading takes place by value request messages. In this case, breakdown on several sites may lead to the ring being split into several 'little' rings, with separate privilege travelling around each of them. Chapter 5 will consider another algorithm (Le Lann 1977), in which privilege is explicitly transmitted between processes.

4.4. An improvement on Lamport (1974): Hehner and Shyamasundar's algorithm (1981)

In this mutual exclusion algorithm (Hehner and Shyamasundar 1981) all processes follow the same protocol to enter the critical section. Each process has a variable associated with it that it can read and modify, but which other processes can only read. This algorithm is very similar to Lamport's, but only uses one variable per process.

> *var number : array* $[0 .. n-1]$ *of integer*;

These variables are initialized to $+\infty$.

The protocol for process P_i is as follows:

> *number* $[i] \leftarrow 0$;
> *number* $[i] \leftarrow 1 + maxfinite$ (*number*);
> *for* $j = 0$ *to* $n-1$, $i \neq j$
>   *wait least* (i, j);

$<$ *critical section* $>$;
number $[i] \leftarrow + \infty$

with the following function and predicate definitions:

least $(i, j) \equiv$ (*number* $[i] <$ *number* $[j]$) $\lor$ (*number* $[i] =$ *number* $[j] \land i < j$)
maxfinite (*number*) $= max$ {(*number* $[i]$: *number* $[i] \neq + \infty$)}

The common feature between this algorithm and Lamport's is that the processes have a number determining the order in which they will later enter the critical section.

As the operation whereby a process selects a number does not take place under mutual exclusion, two processes could take the same number. If this occurs, they are distinguished by their index numbers, and the process with the lower number is arbitrarily admitted first. Behaviour as defined by the protocol is not therefore symmetrical for all processes. Note, however, that this algorithm does use fewer variables than Lamport's — only one per process.

PROOF

We shall use Gries and Owicki's axiomatic technique to prove the validity of this algorithm. The proof is based on the introduction of auxiliary variable $B_{i,j}$, an array of Booleans initialized to true. With *ai* as a local variable in P_i, the protocol then becomes:

```
 1 : number [i] ← 0;
 2 : ai ← 1 + maxfinite (number);
 3 : number [i] ← ai;
 4 : for j = 1 to n − 1 do
 5 :              begin wait least (i, j);
 6 :                   B[i, j] ← false;
 7 :              end enddo;
 8 :               < critical section >;
 9 :               for j = 1 to n do B[i, j] ← true enddo;
10 :               number [i] ← + ∞;
```

We should note first of all that introducing array variable B does not in any way alter the protocol's values or its flow of control, as B has values assigned to it but is never read. This protocol is therefore exactly equivalent to the last one.

We shall start by proving the invariance of predicate I:

$$I = \forall(m, n): B[m, n] \lor least[m, n] \lor number [n] = 0$$

We start by observing that I is true initially ($B[m, n] = true$). We must now show that assignments to *number* and B leave it true.

bu line   1 : sets *number* $[i] = 0$. By the definition of the predicate we now have : $\forall j : least\ (i, j) \lor number\ [j] = 0$ from which we can conclude that $I\ (i, n)$ and $I\ (m, i)$ remain true.

bu line   3 : assigns *number* $[i]$ while $\forall j : B\ [i, j]$. Consequently, I (i, n) remains true. $I\ (m, i)$ is also true because either *least* (m, i) is true, or *least* (m, i) is false, in which case another process P_m has also executed line 3 and we will therefore have $B\ [m, i]$ set to true, which will preserve the invariant.

bu line   6 : as the assignment $B\ [i, j] \leftarrow false$ occurs after waiting for *least* (i, j). $I\ (i, j)$ remains true.

bu line   9 : $I\ (i, j)$ remains true, trivially.

bu line 10: $I\ (i, n)$ remains true because we have executed $B\ [i, n] \leftarrow$ true at line 9 and $I\ (m, i)$ remains true as *least* (m, i) is true.

Having demonstrated this invariant, we go on to prove mutual exclusion by contradiction. If P_i and P_j are simultaneously in their critical sections, we have:

$$number\ [i] \neq 0 \land (\forall k_1 : \lnot B[i, k_1])$$

and *number* $[j]$

and $$\neq 0 \land (\forall k_2 : \lnot B[j, k_2])$$

Setting $k_1 = j$ and $k_2 = i$:

$$number\ [i] \neq 0 \land \lnot B[i, j] \land number\ [j] \neq 0 \land \lnot B[j, i]$$

using the invariant $I\ (m, n)$, we can conclude:

$$least\ (i, j) \land least\ (j, i)$$

which is self-contradictory.

To demonstrate that deadlock is avoided, we need only note that P_i can be blocked only when $\lnot least\ (i, j)$. As the *least* relation is transitive and non-reflexive, it is impossible to form a closed cycle of blocked processes.

What is more, the protocol guarantees fairness: a process P_i may not enter its critical section twice while a process P_j is still waiting. This is because *number* $[j]$ would then be finite and would not change value, since P_i would carry out the assignment *number* $[i] \leftarrow 1 + maxfinite\ (number)$ during its second access to the critical section. We would then have $\lnot\ least\ (i, j)$ and P_i would have to wait for P_j to enter its critical section. Waiting times are therefore linearly limited: $d(n) = n - 1$.

Comment

This protocol is similar to the one proposed by Ricart and Agrawala (1981) for systems using message communication. It represents something of an improvement over Lamport's bakery protocol, discussed in Section 4.2, but suffers from the same disadvantage: there is no limit to the possible growth of the *number* variables. Infinite growth takes place if there is always some process in its critical section. In Section 4.6 we shall see an algorithm that avoids this fault (Peterson 1983a).

4.5. Distributing a centralized algorithm: Kessels' algorithm (1982)

If we consider Peterson's 1981 algorithm for two processes, we notice that variable *turn* is read and updated by both processes P_0 and P_1. Kessels' algorithm (1982) distributes this variable between the two processes in such a way that each of them can read and write its own variable but can only read that of the other process. We shall see that using a distributed variable results in a distributed control algorithm. The necessary variables are:

> *var flag* : *array* [0 .. 1] *of boolean*;
> *turn* : *array* [0 .. 1] *of* 0 .. 1;

The variables are initialized to false and to arbitrary values respectively. The protocol for process P_i is then as follows, with $i = 0$, 1 and $j = i + 1$ *mod* 2.

> *flag* [*i*] ← *true*;
> *turn* [*i*] ← *turn* [*j*] + *i* *mod* 2;
> *wait* (*flag* [*j*] = *false*) ∨ [*turn* [*i*] ≠ (*turn* [*j*] + *i* *mod* 2)];
> < *critical section* >;
> *flag* [*i*] ← *false*;

PROOF

Kessels (1982) gives a formal proof of the validity of this protocol: it guarantees mutual exclusion, avoids deadlock and is fair. We shall use a contradiction argument to prove mutual exclusion, by assuming both P_0 and P_1 to be simultaneously in their critical sections. We then have *flag* [0] = *flag* [1] = *true*. Both processes cannot have entered their critical sections at the same time, or we would have had:

> (*turn* [0] ≠ *turn* [1] + 0 *mod* 2)
> ∧ (*turn* [1] ≠ *turn* [0] + 1 *mod* 2)

Variables *turn* [0 .. 1] are initialized to arbitrary values, so we can evaluate this logical formula in all four possible configurations, whereupon we find that the result is always false.

One process therefore entered its critical section before the other; let us assume that it was P_0. In order to enter its critical section, P_1 must find the following statement true:

> *turn* [1] ≠ *turn* [0] + 1 *mod* 2

which is impossible because it has already assigned this value to *turn* [1] and P_0 has not modified the value of *turn* [0] since that assignment and test, and because it would otherwise either have not been the first to enter its critical section, which contradicts our assumption, or both processes would have entered their critical sections together, which as we have shown is impossible.

Mutual exclusion is therefore guaranteed by this protocol.

We shall leave it as an exercise to the reader to prove that the protocol avoids deadlock and is fair. A formal solution is in Kessels (1982).

THIS ALGORITHM COMPARED WITH OTHERS

As we have already said, this algorithm is a distributed version of Peterson's. Assume that *turn* is initialized to 0; we shall now rewrite the protocols for both processes P_0 and P_1, eliminating the variables *flag* 0 .. 1 in each. We obtain:

for P_0 : *turn* [0] ← *turn* [1];
    wait *turn* [0] ≠ *turn* [1];
    < *critical section* >;

for P_1 : *turn* [1] ← *turn* [0] + 1 ***mod*** 2;
    wait *turn* [1] = *turn* [0];
    < *critical section* >;

It is obvious that as binary variables *turn* [0 .. 1] are either equal or different, if processes begin by waiting (in the second line of the protocol) only one P_i will be able to enter its critical section, which it will release by assigning a new value to *turn* [i]. This will then allow P_j to access its critical section. We then obtain the following new protocols:

for P_0 : ***wait*** *turn* [0] ≠ *turn* [1];
    < *critical section* >;
    turn [0] ← *turn* [1];

for P_1: ***wait*** *turn* [1] = *turn* [0]:
    < *critical section* >;
    turn [1] ← *turn* [0] + 1 ***mod*** 2;

The privileged status allowing a process to enter its critical section is therefore granted in turn to P_0 and P_1. This algorithm is the same as Dijkstra's for the case where $n = k = 2$. In Peterson's and Kessels' algorithms, the *flag* variables therefore avoid a process being blocked when the other does not require access to its critical section.

One way of viewing Kessels' algorithm is to see it as a simplification of Rivest and Pratt's algorithm (1976) for the case of two processes. We shall not discuss the latter here; the reader will find it described in full in the authors' paper.

4.6. Minimizing the number of values used: Peterson's algorithm (1983)

Peterson (1983a) proposes an algorithm that guarantees mutual exclusion, avoidance of deadlock and fairness, but is fairly complex. Its essential property is that for each process it uses variables taking only one of four values, without requiring, as was the case in Dijkstra'a 1974 algorithm, that privilege should travel round a ring. This gets round the problem of potentially unlimited growth of the *number* variables, which was the flaw in Lamport's 1974 algorithm. It is also fault tolerant. With the usual constraints on access to distributed variables, the necessary variables are:

> *var c : array* [0 .. $n-1$] *of* 0 .. 3;

all initialized to 0.

We shall describe the protocol in stages, following a top-down approach, to make it easier to understand. For P_i (where $i = 0 \ldots n - 1$) we have the following protocol:

> *clock-code*;
> *conflict-code*;
> < *critical section* >;
> $c[i] \leftarrow 0$;

We shall start by looking at *conflict-code*.

> *conflict-code* $s \leftarrow c[i]$;
> > **repeat**
> > **begin** $c[i] \leftarrow s$;
> >   *wait* $\forall j > i : c[j] \neq 3$;
> > $c[i] \leftarrow 3$;
> > **end**;
> > **until** $\forall j > i : c[j] \neq 3$;
> > *wait* $\forall j < i : c[j] \neq 3$;

PROOF

This part of the protocol guarantees mutual exclusion. In order to enter its critical section, process P_i must be the only process for which $c[i] = 3$. Consequently, if P_i is in its critical section, P_j, seeing $c[i] = 3$, will not be able to enter its critical section; what is more, two processes will not be able to enter their critical sections simultaneously, as is made clear by the final two conditions.

We now assume that *clock-code* prevents any process P_j, with $j > i$, moving from its non-critical section through *clock-code* to *conflict-code*, as long as P_i is in its *conflict-code*. *Clock-code* uses values 1 and 2 for $c[i]$, whereas *conflict-code* uses 3.

On this assumption, no process may be blocked in *conflict-code*. We are not going to prove the fact formally. We only observe that the first two wait conditions for P_i block it with $c[i] \neq 3$ until all processes P_j for which $j > i$ have left their critical section; P_i will then exit the *repeat* loop, and will wait until all processes P_j, with $(j < i) \wedge c[j] = 3$, have released their critical sections. While waiting in this way, it can only be overtaken by processes P_j $(j > i)$ and the assumptions we have made imply that this can only happen a finite number of times, by processes already in *clock-code*.

Formal proof is by induction, showing initially that P_{n-1} cannot be indefinitely blocked, which is trivially true, then that as P_{n-1} to P_{i+1} cannot be indefinitely blocked, the same is true for P_i.

On the assumptions we have made, neither deadlock nor starvation can therefore take place.

THE ALGORITHM (CONT.)

We still need to supply the *clock-code* part of the prelude. In particular, it has to satisfy the assumption we made above. The idea governing its design is that a process P_i may be on one of two 'sides': $c[i] = 1$ or $c[i] = 2$. A process attempting to enter its critical section starts by moving to one side or the other, depending on which processes are already present, and must change sides twice in a row before it can enter *conflict-code*. Choosing a side and changing sides are governed by the following rules, which make our assumption true:

```
clock-code : position (i);
             change (i);
             change (i);
```

Function *position* assigns a side $c[i] = 1$ or $c[i] = 2$ to P_i as follows, where *result* indicates a returned value:

```
function position (i); integer i;
  begin
    for h from i − 1 to 0 step − 1 do
    begin
      t ← c [h];
      if t = 1 ∨ t = 3 then result 1
      elsif t = 2 then result 2;
    end;
    for h = n − 1 to i step − 1 do
    begin
      t ← c [h];
      if t = 1 ∨ t = 3 then result 2
      elsif t = 2 then result 1;
```

end;
   result 1;
end;

Function *position* returns 1 or 2 as its result: it scans variables $c[i]$ in the processes as if they were on a logical ring $P_{i-1}, ..., P_1, P_0, P_{n-1}, P_{n-2}, ..., P_i$. If a process P_j such that $j < i$ (to the left on the ring) is a candidate for privilege, then $c[i]$ has the same value as $c[j]$; if there is no such process, we look to see whether there is a P_j, with $j > i$, in which case $c[i]$ has the 'opposite' side from $c[j]$. If P_i is the only process in question, then $c[i] = 1$.

As we have now determined a rule for assigning a 'side', we can now go on to state the rule for changing sides: a process P_i can change sides only if all processes P_j, with $j < i$, are on the other side; if the process is P_1, or if none of the processes P_j with lower index number is interested in mutual exclusion, i.e. $c[j] = 0$, then P_i can only change side if while scanning processes from P_{n-1} towards P_i it finds a P_k such that $c[k] = c[i]$. As long as neither of these conditions applies, P_i cannot change sides. The change takes place by executing the statement $c[i] \leftarrow 3 - c[i]$.

```
procedure change (i); integer i;
    begin
WL : wait c [i] ≠ position (i);
        for h from 0 to i − 1 step 1 do
            begin
                t ← c [h];
                if c [i] = t ∨ t = 3 then go to WL;
            end;
        c [i] ← 3 − c [i];
    end;
```

Peterson (1983a) showed that a process P_i cannot constantly change sides, and cannot be permanently prevented from executing *change* (i); moreover, it can only change sides twice in a row if a process P_j such that $j < i$ has changed sides beforehand. This verifies the assumption we made earlier. A process P_j must execute *change* (j) twice before entering *conflict-code*. But all processes P_i, with $i < j$, that are in *conflict-code* have $c[i]$ set either to a fixed value or to 3. If P_j finds $c = 3$, it waits; moreover, if it is to execute *change* $[j]$ twice, its loop condition makes it wait for all the P_i such that $i < j$ to have changed side, i.e. changed the value of their $c[i]$, which they can only do in *conflict-code*. Consequently, no process not in the protocol may enter its *conflict-code* if there is a process P_i in this code with $i < j$.

THE ALGORITHM

For process P_i we can therefore finally draw up the following protocol:

```
c [i] ← position (i);
change (i);
change (i);
s ← c [i];
repeat begin
        c [i] ← s;
        wait ∀ j > i : c [j] ≠ 3;
        c [i] ← 3;
    end;
until ∀ j > i : c [j] ≠ 3;
wait ∀ j < i : c [j] ≠ 3;
< critical section >;
c [i] ← 0;
```

Chapter 5

The mutual exclusion problem in a distributed framework: solutions based on message communication

5.1. Introduction

This chapter is concerned with mutual exclusion algorithms based on the communication of messages between processes. These processes have only local variables, and the only way they can exchange information with each other is by communicating it explicitly.

The algorithms based on state variables seen in the last chapter could be implemented using a system of messages. However, the fundamental difference between those algorithms and the ones considered in this chapter is that here the messages are of 'send information' rather than 'request information' type: every time a process changes its state, it broadcasts information concerning its new state to the processes that make up its environment — the other processes never request this information. Each of these two forms of message may, of course, be viewed as the complement of the other, but it is clear that messages of the kind with which we shall be concerned in this chapter have major advantages over the other type: the number of messages transmitted are kept down to a minimum, there are no messages exchanged for no purpose, and all messages carried by the system correspond to state changes in the processes.

We do not consider the concept of a distributed algorithm to include approaches where a control process exists to which all other processes submit requests for entry into, and information concerning their release of, the critical section. Such an approach, although formally depending on the use of messages, is, in fact, a centralized algorithm: failure of the control process has exactly the same effect as failure of variable *turn* used in centralized algorithms, in that it leads to breakdown of the algorithm as a whole. This is not, of course, to say that such a non-distributed algorithm may be of some value, depending on the architectural characteristics of the system on which it is to be run.

We shall make no distinction, in this chapter, between the concept of a process as it has been used in previous chapters and the concept of a site in the distributed architecture. In most of these algorithms, there will be two processes at each site that may enter into competition for a critical section: one of the processes will be responsible for the activity carried on at that site, and will therefore emit requests for entry into the critical section, while the other will be responsible for receiving messages transmitted by other sites and making the necessary assignments to variables local to its own site. These two centralized processes on the same site may enter into competition for access to the variables local to the site, in which case the mechanisms discussed in Chapters 2 and 3 will be used to resolve any conflict between them.

5.2. A token on a logical ring: Le Lann's algorithm (1977)

A simple way of implementing mutual exclusion in a distributed system is to pass a special mark (for which the term token or privilege is often used) around the processes: the process holding the token may enter its critical section. It is self-evident that if there is only one token, mutual exclusion is guaranteed, and if the processes forming the distributed system are connected by a unidirectional logical ring structure, the exclusion protocol will avoid deadlock and guarantee fairness. For process P_i, such a protocol, as proposed by Le Lann (1977), is:

> **wait** (*token*) **from** P_{i-1};
> < *critical section* >;
> **send** (*token*) **to** P_{i+1};

Any physical communication network can be used: as long as all the processes are connected, it is always possible to implement a logical ring structure.

As the ring is unidirectional, starvation cannot take place, but the number of messages necessary to implement exclusion can go from 1 (in the case where all processes are attempting to enter the critical section) to infinity (in the case where no process is attempting to enter it).

FAULT TOLERANCE

There are two types of breakdown that can affect this algorithm: loss of the token and the breakdown of a process.

In cases of process breakdown, a new logical ring must be established. It is generally left to the transport system to provide every site P_i with two state variables:

> **var** *neighbour* [(*left*, *right*), i]: $0 .. n - 1$;

and it is generally up to the system to update them if a site breaks down. Variables are initialized to:

> *neighbour* [*left*, i] ← $i - 1$ **mod** n;
> *neighbour* [*right*, i] ← $i + 1$ **mod** n;

Further details on reconfiguring this kind of ring can be found in Section 4.3, where we discussed an algorithm by Dijkstra (1974) based on the use of state variables, in which the problem is fundamentally similar, and where mutual suspicion and systematic acknowledgement protocols are used to make reconfiguration possible.

What, however, happens if the token is lost (see Le Lann 1978)? To solve this problem, each site is provided with redundant information.

The token has a value v between 0 and $k - 1$. [This value can, incidentally, also be used to implement a circulating sequencer mechanism (Cornafion 1981).] Each site P_i is provided with a state variable:

var state $[i]$ $: 0 .. k - 1;$

and executes the following actions before retransmitting the token:

if $i = 0$ *then* $v \leftarrow v + 1$ *mod k endif*;
state $[i] \leftarrow v;$

As can clearly be seen, the effect of these actions is to keep the token moving round the ring at the end of each site's turn, and to store the last value read. Each time the token passes through site P_i, it sets a safety clock running. If the preset time limit is exceeded before the token returns, P_i consults the state variable of its predecessor P_j, where $j = neighbour$ $[left, i]$. If one or other of the following conditions is true:

$(j > i \wedge state\ [j] = state\ [i])$
$(j < i \wedge state\ [j] \neq state\ [i])$

the token is regarded as lost. Site P_i regenerates it, giving it the correct value, *state* $[j]$, and sets the safety clock running again. This fault tolerance protocol is described in Le Lann (1978). As is clear from the tests made of state variable *state* $[i]$, the token must be able to take at least two distinct values $k \geqslant 2$, for the algorithm to operate correctly. Its advantage is its simplicity. If we do not want to use a token with values, we can instead use a protocol based on defining a coordinating process whose responsibility is to regenerate a token if it gets lost, but this leads to the problem of what happens if the coordinating process breaks down. In this case, an algorithm has to be executed to decide which process will be the new coordinator, and algorithms of this kind are called election algorithms. There are several such algorithms, all of them essentially similar: one such algorithm would assign a different number to every process, and the coordinator is the one with the highest number (Le Lann 1977).

To conclude our remarks on algorithms based on token-passing, it is worth pointing out that this protocol is analogous to 'daisy chaining' or 'polling' techniques used respectively for bus sharing or for sharing a server station between several terminal stations. It is also similar to the use of 'round-robin' techniques for the fair sharing of resources.

5.3. Distributing a queue: Lamport's algorithm (1978)

The first wholly distributed solution that imposes no *a priori* order on the way in which privilege moves from process to process was developed by Lamport (1978). His work is based on two crucial components. On the one hand, a basic mechanism: dating of system events (transmission and reception of messages) using a message timestamping process. On the other hand, there is a new methodological approach: the distribution of a single queue over several sites.

THE TIMESTAMPING MECHANISM

One of the problems involved in a distributed algorithm is the way in which messages are ordered, i.e. of establishing a total order between all the events in the system. To make this possible, every message is given a number by its transmitter, called its timestamp or logical date. This number is the value of a (logical) clock local to the transmission site. Local clocks may run at different rates, and they have to be reset from time to time: this is done when processes communicate with each other. At each process or site P_i, we therefore have a local clock declaration:

var c_i : 0 .. + ∞;

Between any two successive events at site P_i, the site increments its clock:

$c_i \leftarrow c_i + 1$;

When a message is transmitted by P_i to P_j, P_i stamps the message with a value of c and transmits the triplet (*message*, c_i, i) to P_j.

When site P_j receives a message stamped c, it resets its own clock if it is running slow, as follows:

if $c_j < c$ *then* $c_j \leftarrow c$ *endif*;

and P_j then dates the message receipt event as follows:

$c_j \leftarrow c_j + 1$;

With these rules for timestamp management, transmission always precedes reception of the corresponding message. It is, however, possible that two independent events could have the same date. If we want to arrange them according to a total ordering, we only have to do a topological sort on the partial ordering defined by the timestamps, by adding an arbitrary rule: two events with the same datestamp are ordered by the numbers of their sites; the fact that the rule is arbitrary is without importance, as the events are independent.

We shall therefore say that event E_1, which occurred on site i and is dated $c_i(E_1)$, precedes E_2, which occurred on site j and is dated $c_j(E_2)$, if and only if:

$$c_i\ (E_1)\ <\ c_j\ (E_2)\ \lor\ [c_i\ (E_1) = c_j\ (E_2)\ \land\ i\ <\ j]$$

There are other timestamping mechanisms that have similar properties (see Andre et al. 1985 or Kaneko et al. 1979). Kaneko et al. in particular guarantee that the difference between two clocks will never be greater than 1.

THE BASIS OF THE ALGORITHM: DISTRIBUTING A QUEUE

A simple way of implementing mutual exclusion would be to define an allocation process for the critical section. It would manage a queue updated by critical section request and release messages. Messages would be held in the queue in the order of their arrival, and the allocation process would serve them in that order. In order to distribute this centralized algorithm, we need to distribute the queue over all the sites, i.e. we need to manage a copy of the queue on each site. This means that every site must receive all the request and release messages from all other sites. To eliminate problems associated with asynchronism between processes and the speed of transmission of messages — although it has to be said that we make the assumption that messages cannot overtake each other between two sites — messages are totally ordered using the unique timestamp mechanism discussed above. All the sites therefore see the messages arranged in the same order. For a process to take a decision based only on its own queue, it needs, moreover, to have received a message that is not 'too old' from each of the other processes, in order to guarantee that no message earlier than any of the others is still in transit to it. This is the underlying principle on which the algorithm is based.

THE ALGORITHM

We shall now describe the protocol that implements this algorithm. The following type declarations are common to all sites:

> *type clock* : $0\ ..\ +\ \infty$;
>   *sitenum* : $0\ ..\ n-1$;
>   *mestyp* : (*req, ack, rel*);

The meaning of these different types of messages is as follows:

— When a process is attempting to enter its critical section it broadcasts a message of the *req* type to all the other processes.

— When it leaves its critical section it broadcasts a message of the *rel* type.

— When a process P_j has received a message of the *req* type from P_i, it acknowledges receipt with an *ack* — it is this that implements the concept of a 'not too old' message, which we mentioned earlier.

Every process has a local clock and transmits messages made up of three fields:

(type of message, local clock, site number)

So the message carries not only its own meaning but also the necessary information to ensure that the timing mechanism remains coherent. Every process maintains a queue that has entries for processes containing such messages. We therefore have the following local declarations for each process P_i:

> **var** *osn* : *clock*;
> *q* : **array** $[0 .. n - 1]$ *of message*;

Clock *osn* is managed as before: if it runs slow, it is reset on receiving a new message in such a way as to ensure that every transmission date is earlier than any receipt date.

The queue is managed as follows. At any instant, entry $q[j]$ contains a message from P_j; initially we have:

> $q\ [j] = (rel,\ 0,\ j)$

When a message is broadcast by P_i, it is also recorded in $q[i]$. Updating $q[j]$ by P_i takes place as follows:

— On receipt of a message $(req,\ k,\ j)$ or $(rel,\ k,\ j)$, it is recorded in $q[j]$. It should be remembered that receipt by P_i of a message of the $(req,\ k,\ j)$ type triggers the transmission of a message of the $(ack,\ osn,\ i)$ type from P_i to P_j.

— On receipt of a message $(ack,\ k,\ j)$ it is placed in $q[j]$ if that entry does not contain a message of the $(req,\ k,\ j)$ type, otherwise the message is ignored.

A process P_i enters the critical section when q contains a *req* type message, and its timestamp is the oldest, since then its request has precedence over all the others. (Recall that q contains messages from all sites).

The protocol for P_i can be presented in two parts, one concerned with message receipt, the other with requests for entry into the critical section. It will then take the following form, which also covers management of the local queue on the site and of the local clock.

> **broadcast** $(req,\ osn,\ i)$;
> $q\ [i] \leftarrow (req,\ osn,\ i)$; $osn \leftarrow osn + 1$;
> **wait** $\forall\ j \neq i$ *timestamp* $(q[i]) <$ *timestamp* $(q[j])$;
> $<$ *critical section* $>$;
> **broadcast** $(rel,\ osn,\ i)$;
> $q\ [i] \leftarrow (rel,\ osn,\ i)$; $osn \leftarrow osn + 1$;
>
> **on receipt**
>   **of** $(req,\ k,\ j)$ **do begin** *update* $(osn,\ k)$;
> $q\ [j] \leftarrow (req,\ k,\ j)$;
>   *send* $(ack,\ osn,\ i)$ *to j*;
>   **end**;

of (*rel*, *k*, *j*) *do* **begin** *update* (*osn*, *k*);
                q [*j*] ← (*rel*, *k*, *j*);
         end ;
of (*ack*, *k*, *j*) *do* **begin** *update* (*osn*, *k*);
                if type of (*q*[*j*]) ≠ *req*
                then q [*j*] ← (*ack*, *k*, *j*);
                endif;
         end ;

Function *timestamp* returns fields *clock* and *site number* of *q*[*j*], and operator < is defined on pairs of integers as follows (cf. Chapter 4, Section 4.2, the bakery algorithm):

$$(a, b) < (c, d) \equiv (a < c) \vee [(a = c) \wedge (b < d)]$$

Procedure *update* is responsible for updating the local clock of a process following the procedure described above:

procedure *update* (*osn*, *k* : *clock*);
    begin
        if *osn* < *k* **then** *osn* ← *k* **endif**;
        osn ← *osn* + 1;
    end ;

PROOF

Requests for entry into the critical section are handled according to the total ordering between messages imposed by the datestamping mechanism. Once P_i decides to enter its critical section, there can be no other message of the *req* type in the system that was transmitted before its own, for P_i has by then necessarily received a message from all other sites and these messages date from later than its own *req* message. (We can be sure of this because of the *ack* message mechanism; it should be remembered that messages between two sites cannot overtake each other.) Note too that site P_i can save itself the transmission of an *ack* message to P_j if P_i has sent a *req* message but has not yet received the corresponding *rel* message.

The protocol is therefore fair and avoids deadlock — the total ordering relation between messages is acyclic. Mutual exclusion is also guaranteed because the process that is in its critical section will only delete the *req* message in the queues of other processes, which are therefore in the meantime prevented from entering their critical sections by the timestamping mechanism, once it has left its own critical section and transmitted the *rel* message.

As a measure of the efficiency of this algorithm, it is worth observing that to guarantee exclusion in this way we need $3(n - 1)$ messages, where n is the number of sites.

FAULT TOLERANCE

The above protocol was improved in Cornafion (1981) to make it more fault-tolerant. Breakdown in a process P_i will not be fatal for the algorithm if it takes place while P_i is not in its critical section: it is then only necessary to broadcast a special message (*absent*, k, i) to all other sites. The critical section entry tests for P_i need therefore only be made for entries in the queue containing messages whose type is different from *absent*:

$$wait\ j \neq i : (type\ q\ [j] \neq absent)$$
$$\Rightarrow datestamp\ (q\ [i]) < datestamp\ (q\ [j])$$

If process P_i is in its critical section and breaks down, the transport network must broadcast the message (*absent*, $+ \infty$, i). When a process wishes to rejoin the system after a breakdown, it must update the state of its own queue and indicate its presence to all the other processes. To do so it can broadcast a special message *reentry* to all the other processes P_i, to which each of them replies with its last not yet satisfied *req* message if there is one, otherwise with a *rel* message. The transport network must reply with an *absent* message for all broken down sites. Once it has received all the replies to its *reentry* message, P_i can return to normal behaviour.

5.4. Pursuit of optimality: Ricart and Agrawala's algorithm (1981)

The algorithm proposed by Ricart and Agrawala (1981) sets out to minimize the number of messages necessary for mutual exclusion. It can be viewed as an optimization of Lamport's in which messages of the acknowledgement type relating to a request for entry into the critical section have been eliminated. The algorithm assumes the presence of a transport network free of errors, in which the transit time of messages may vary and messages may overtake each other. It requires $2(n-1)$ messages to implement exclusion, i.e. $n-1$ to indicate P_i's intention of entering its critical section to the other processes, and a further $n-1$ to carry the favourable replies necessary to allow the access it has requested.

THE PRINCIPLE OF THE ALGORITHM

When a process P_i wishes to enter its critical section, it generates a timestamp — with a timing mechanism analogous to that used by Lamport — and broadcasts a message to all the other processes of the *req* type, accompanied by this timestamp. When a process P_j receives such a message, it may either reply favourably by sending back a *rep* type message straight away or defer its response. A process that has received a reply message from every other process may enter its critical section. On leaving its critical section, a process sends any deferred *rep* messages to all processes awaiting such a reply. A decision to reply at once or to delay its reply to a request message is based on a priority mechanism between processes defined by the following rules: if a process does not wish to enter its critical section, it sends a favourable reply at once; if it wants to enter its critical section, it compares the timestamp of its request with that of the last request received, and if the latter is more recent — which, as defined by the total ordering relation between timestamps, means that its value is greater — it decides to defer its reply, otherwise *rep* is sent at once.

THE ALGORITHM

The protocol implementing this algorithm requires a certain number of declarations local to each of the processes $P_1, ..., P_i, ..., P_n$. For P_i these are:

> *var osn* : $0 .. + \infty$;
> *hsn* : $0 .. + \infty$;
> *numrepexpected* : $0 .. n - 1$;
> *csrequested* : *boolean*;
> *repdeferred* : **array** $[1 .. n]$ **of** *boolean*;
> *priority* : *boolean*;

Variables *osn* and *hsn* respectively represent the sequence number chosen by P_i to timestamp its own request, and the largest number in the sequence perceived by P_i in a request; *hsn*, initialized to 0, is used to update the timestamping 'clock' *osn*. Booleans are initialized to false; *repdeferred* $[j]$ is true if P_i has deferred its reply to a request from P_j.

As before, we shall present this protocol in two parts: the first is directly concerned with requests for mutual exclusion from P_i, and the second with updating local variables in P_i on receipt of messages from other sites. The two parts can be executed simultaneously, but access to variables must be protected by an exclusion mechanism, which we have deliberately left out of our presentation for the sake of clarity.

> *csrequested* $\leftarrow$ *true*;
> *osn* $\leftarrow$ *hsn* + 1;
> *numrepexpected* $\leftarrow$ $n - 1$;
> **for** $j \neq i, j \in 1 .. n$
>   **send** (*req*, *osn*, *i*) *to* j;
> **wait** (*numrepexpected* = 0);
> < *critical section* >;
> *csrequested* $\leftarrow$ *false*;
> **for** $j = 1$ **to** n **do**
>   **if** *repdeferred* $[j]$ **then begin**
>   *repdeferred* $[j]$ $\leftarrow$ *false*;

$$send \; (rep) \; to \; j \;;$$
$$end \;;$$

      endif ;
    on receipt
      of (*req*, *k*, *j*) *do*

               begin
                   hsn ← *max* (*hsn*, *k*);
                   priority ← *csrequested* ∧
$$[(k > osn) \lor (k = osn \land i < j)] \;;$$
                   if priority then repdeferred [*j*] ← *true*
                              else send (*rep*) *to j*
                 endif ;
               end ;
      of (*rep*)   *do numrepexpected* ← *numrepexpected* − 1;

PROOF

We shall start by showing the exclusion property: for any pair of processes, one must leave the critical section before the other can enter it. Assume that two processes P_i and P_j are simultaneously in their critical sections, and consider the message traffic just before this occurs: each process has transmitted a message *rep* towards the other and has received from it a favourable reply *rep*. Various cases can then appear.

(1) P_i has sent its reply to a request from P_j before selecting the *osn* stamp for its request message. That stamp will therefore necessarily be greater than the stamp on the request from P_j. Consequently when P_j receives the request message from P_i — at which stage the value of its variable *csrequested* = *true* — it will defer its reply, and it will therefore be impossible for both processes P_i and P_j to be in their critical sections simultaneously.

(2) Another possible case is the symmetrical situation between P_i and P_j, and the consequences are the same.

(3) The third case is that each process sends a reply to the other after having transmitted its timestamped request. Each process will therefore find its Boolean *csrequested* = *true*, when it receives the request from the other process, since updating takes place before a request is sent. Each process will therefore compare the timestamps on the requests, and as these are totally ordered, only one *priority* Boolean will be false, making it possible to send a favourable reply. This therefore implies the exclusion property.

The algorithm also avoids deadlock: the critical section is always attainable if at least one process is attempting to enter it. To prove this let us assume the opposite: no process can enter its critical section because it is still awaiting favourable replies. Once there are no further messages in transit, and if this situation continues, there must be a cycle amongst the processes, where each has transmitted a request to its successor while that successor has not replied. This situation, however, cannot arise, since a decision to defer a reply is based on a relation that totally orders requests. There is therefore one request that has the earliest timestamp, and which will receive all the necessary favourable replies. Deadlock is therefore impossible.

In the same way, starvation cannot take place. As requests are totally ordered, they are served in that order: every request will at some stage become the oldest, and will then be served.

Note that this algorithm resembles the one proposed by Hehner and Shyamasundar (1981), which we examined in Section 4.4. Proofs of deadlock avoidance and of non-starvation are the same: they depend on the total ordering relation provided by the timestamping mechanism.

NUMBER OF MESSAGES

The protocol requires $2(n-1)$ messages for each entry into a critical section: $n-1$ are for request messages, and the same number is required for favourable replies. The authors show that this number is the minimum for processes acting independently, concurrently executing a distributed and symmetric algorithm.

If the maximum transmission delay between two sites is known, a modification can be made to the protocol. The meaning of a reply is reversed, so that no reply during the maximum delay period implies a favourable response, and a message of the *delayed* type is explicitly sent to indicate an unfavourable reply. The number of messages necessary for each entry into a critical section then varies between $n-1$ and $3(n-1)$, depending on the number of *delayed* messages sent. (Sending such a message implies that a favourable reply will have to be sent later.)

By similar reasoning, we can see that if the processes are arranged in a ring, n messages will be sufficient.

THE EFFECT OF ORDERING THE MESSAGES

The length of time a process waits before entering its critical section depends on whether or not messages are received in the order in which they are transmitted. To calculate the upper limit to this delay, let us first of all assume that the order of messages is not preserved.

Consider a process P_n, for which priority is always unfavourable whenever there is a conflict owing to equality between timestamps. We observe that the maximum difference between the timestamp for P_n and the minimum timestamp is $n-1$. If a careful choice is made for the order in which messages are received — messages of the *rep* type overtake messages of the *req* type — it is possible for a process to enter its critical section a number of times, which equals the difference between its own current timestamp and that of P_n. At worst, all processes have a different timestamp. One of them therefore will be able to enter its critical section n times before P_n, another $n - 1$ times, etc. The maximum delay is therefore

$$d_1(n) = \frac{n(n + 1)}{2} - 1$$

In cases where messages are received in the order in which they are transmitted — i.e. they cannot overtake each other — a process may not enter its critical section more than twice in succession if another is also attempting to enter it (once because its timestamp is older, and once more because its site number is smaller). The limit therefore becomes

$$d_2(n) = 2(n - 1)$$

The interested reader should refer to the appendix in Ricart and Agrawala (1981). It is interesting to compare these limits with those applicable, in a centralized implementation, to the algorithms proposed by De Bruijn (1967) and by Eisenberg and McGuire (1972), which we examined in Chapter 2.

5.5. Minimizing the number of messages: Carvalho and Roucairol's algorithm (1981)

Carvalho and Roucairol's algorithm (1983a), first presented in Carvalho and Roucairol (1981), is an improved version of Ricart and Agrawala's. Ricart and Agrawala consider their own as optimal 'in the sense that a symmetrical, distributed algorithm cannot use fewer messages if requests are processed by each node concurrently'. Their definition of symmetry assumes that any process is warned of any request for entry to the critical section issued by any other process (Ricart and Agrawala 1983, Section 4.1). Carvalho and Roucairol's algorithm uses a different definition of symmetry, which we also find in Burns (1981), which is based on the texts of the processes rather than on their behaviour and thus on their requests.

The assumptions made about the communication medium are the same as for Ricart and Agrawala's algorithm. Summarized briefly, these are that all exchanges of information take place by message, and that the communication medium is error-free but can alter the order between messages on a link between processes.

THE PRINCIPLE OF THE ALGORITHM

It should be remembered that we make no distinction between a process and the site on which it is located. The fundamental idea on which the proposed improvement is based is that if a process P_i has received a favourable response from process P_j, the implicit permission that P_j has just granted to P_i for it to enter its critical section remains valid until P_i sends P_j a favourable response, which cannot happen until P_j has sent a request message to P_i. Between the moment P_j sends an authorization to P_i and the moment at which it sends it a request message, P_i may enter its critical section as often as it wishes. Consequently, once a process has had $n-1$ authorizations, it may enter its critical section without any request or release message being used, for as long as no other process wishes to do so.

The number of messages necessary therefore varies between 0 and $2(n-1)$, and both limits may be reached in practice.

As for symmetry, the text of all processes is identical, but unlike Ricart and Agrawala's algorithm, requests are not handled in parallel by all nodes. In Section 5.6, we shall consider another algorithm based on the same definition of symmetry that uses only n messages (Ricart and Agrawala 1983). This algorithm is therefore parallel, 'symmetric' and distributed.

THE ALGORITHM

The protocol implementing the algorithm uses declarations local to each of the processes $P_1, \ldots, P_i \ldots, P_n$. These are:

```
var osn : .. + ∞;
    hsn : 0 .. + ∞;
    auth : array [1 .. n] of boolean;
    inside : boolean;
    waiting : boolean;
    repdeferred : array [1 .. n] of boolean;
    priority : boolean;
```

Counters *osn* and *hsn* are used as in Ricart and Agrawala, to represent the sequence number — or logical clock — that P_i needs to timestamp its request, and the largest sequence number ever seen by P_i in a request. Both are initialized to 0.

Booleans *waiting* and *inside* are initialized to false, and set to true whenever P_i is waiting or in its critical section, as appropriate. The elements of arrays *auth* [j] and *repdeferred* [j] are *true* respectively when P_i has had a favourable reply from P_j and has not yet sent it a favourable reply, and when P_i is delaying its return of a favourable reply to P_j which has in turn submitted a request to it.

Boolean *priority* shows that whether or not P_i, which has just received a request from P_j, has priority; priority is calculated by comparing timestamps and site numbers.

The prelude and postlude of the critical section, like the actions taken on receipt of messages sent by another process, are indivisible except for the instruction **wait**. An exclusion semaphore may be used to implement that indivisibility, but we have deliberately left this out for the sake of clarity. The protocol for P_i is as follows:

```
waiting ← true;
osn ← hsn + 1;
for j ≠ i, j ∈ 1 .. n do
            if ¬ auth [j] then send (req, osn, i) to j endif;
wait (∀ j ≠ i : auth [j]);
inside ← true;
waiting ← false;
< critical section >;
inside ← false;
for j ≠ i, j ∈ 1 .. n do
            if repdeferred [j] then begin auth [j] ← false;
                                     repdeferred [j] ← false;
                                     send (rep, i) to j;
                                  end;
            endif;
on receipt
    of (rep, j) do auth [j] ← true;
    of (req, k, j) do
begin
            hsn ← max (hsn, k);
            priority ← [(k > osn) ∨ (k = osn ∧ j > i)];
            if inside ∨ (waiting ∧ priority)
                then repdeferred [j] ← true endif;
            if ¬ (inside ∨ waiting)
              ∨ (waiting ∧ ¬ auth [j] ∧ ¬ priority)
                then begin
                        auth [j] ← false;
                        send (rep, i) to j;
                     end;
            endif ;
            if    waiting ∧ auth [j] ∧ ¬ priority
                then begin
                        auth [j] ← false;
                        send (rep, i) to j;
                        send (req, osn, i) to j;
                        end;
            endif;
    end;
```

Comment

(a) This algorithm guarantees mutual exclusion, avoidance of deadlock and avoidance of starvation. We shall give no proof of these properties, as the necessary demonstrations are very similar to those given for Ricart and Agrawala's algorithm.

(b) We shall, however, briefly consider the use of the timestamping mechanism using variable *osn*, whose monotonically increasing value accompanies messages of the *req* type. Unlike Ricart and Agrawala's algorithm, or Lamport's, in which requests are handled in the order of their timestamps, this is no longer the case here. If a process P_j should send a *req* message to P_i, but before receiving it P_i enters its critical section, the order of entry will not be that of their timestamps. Timestamps are only used to sort out priority conflicts between processes. (This is the role of the Boolean *priority*.)

TOWARDS A FORMAL DERIVATION OF THE ALGORITHM

Carvalho and Roucairol (1981) present this algorithm as the distribution of an assertion. Using the following notation:

$$inside_i = true \Leftrightarrow \text{process } P_i \text{ is in its}$$
$$\text{critical section}$$
$$auth_i [j] = true \Leftrightarrow \text{permission has been}$$
$$\text{received from } P_j \text{ by } P_i$$

The problem then becomes one of deriving a solution that satisfies the following invariants:

$$I_1 \ \forall \ i, j : i \neq j \Rightarrow \urcorner \ (inside_i \wedge inside_j)$$
$$I_2 \ \forall \ i, j : inside \Rightarrow auth_i [j]$$
$$I_3 \ \forall \ i, j : i \neq j \Rightarrow \urcorner \ (auth_i [j] \wedge auth_j [i])$$

If I_2 and I_3 are respected, I_1 must necessarily be respected. Invariant I_2 is entirely local. In I_3, however, variables are involved from several processes. The need to respect I_3 generates rules governing the transfer of messages of the *rep* type (the messages that lead to updating $auth_i [j] \leftarrow true$):

(1) P_i cannot set $auth_i [j] \leftarrow true$ unless it has received (*rep*, *j*).
(2) P_j may not **send** (*rep*, *j*) **to** *i* until it has set $auth_j [i] \leftarrow false$.
(3) Two *rep* messages cannot be sent simultaneously by P_i to P_j and by P_j to P_i.

Rules 1 and 2 are easily implemented. As for rule 3 — which, in fact, guarantees mutual exclusion — we will need to look at the various cases that can arise, depending on the states of the processes, and Boolean *priority* is introduced to resolve possible conflicts between requests.

By way of concluding our discussion of this algorithm, it is worth noting two major points that distinguish it from Lamport's or Ricart and Agrawala's algorithms:

— The number of messages necessary for exclusion varies between 0 and $2(n-1)$.

— Although it produces a total ordering, timestamping is only used to resolve conflicts between requests — the order in which processes access their critical section need not be that of their requests.

These two aspects derive from the same cause: the fact that in Ricart and Agrawala's algorithm any request is necessarily associated with a reply (processes wait until all the replies have been received before entering their critical sections) and therefore all local clocks are 'synchronized' *modulo* $(n - 1)$, which is not the case in Carvalho and Roucairol's algorithm.

5.6. Further optimization: Suzuki and Kasami (1982) or Ricart and Agrawala (1983)

SUZUKI AND KASAMI'S APPROACH

Within the same assumptions — an error-free communication medium that does not guarantee that the order of messages between transmitter and receiver is preserved — Suzuki and Kasami study an optimality theory for mutual exclusion algorithms within networks (Suzuki and Kasami 1982). In particular, they examine three ways of measuring the properties of algorithms:

— path models followed by messages (precedence relations);

— the number of messages necessary for exclusion;

— the number of distinct messages.

We have already seen that the number of messages necessary for exclusion is:

— $3(n - 1)$ in Lamport's algorithm;

— $2(n - 1)$ in Ricart and Agrawala's algorithm;

— between 0 and $2(n - 1)$ in Carvalho and Roucairol's algorithm.

Although these numbers are finite, this is not the case for the number of distinct messages that these algorithms may generate. The timestamping mechanism may generate ordinal numbers between 0 and infinity, so, as all messages are timestamped, the number of distinct messages is not *a priori* limited.

In Ricart and Agrawala's algorithm, requests are serviced in the order of their timestamps, and the difference between the local clocks *osn* cannot therefore exceed $n - 1$. Therefore, as these authors point out (Ricart and Agrawala 1981, Section 6.4), although there is no limit to the value that *osn* may take, the range within which it may vary at any given instant is limited: the ordinal numbers vary between x and $x + n - 1$. They can therefore be stored *mod m*, where $m \geqslant 2n - 1$. Whenever two ordinal numbers are compared, the smaller is incremented by m if their difference is greater than or equal to n. $Log_2 (2n - 1)$ bits are therefore necessary and sufficient to hold the timestamps, and the number of distinct messages generated by the algorithm is finite, $2n^2 + 1$.

The same is not true for Carvalho and Roucairol's algorithm (1981), in which the total ordering defined by the timestamping mechanism is not necessarily respected. This means that there is no predefined limit to the maximum difference between the local clocks *osn*. The number of distinct messages is therefore potentially infinite. Note that it is the systematic association between each *req* message and a *rep* message that ensures 'synchronism' of local clocks in Ricart and Algrawala's algorithm, and as this association is not guaranteed here, the two algorithms behave differently.

We now return to Suzuki and Kasami (1982). They propose three versions of an algorithm, which differ by the number of messages necessary to implement exclusion and by the number of distinct messages. The basic algorithm needs n and a potentially infinite number, respectively. The other two versions optimize the initial algorithm using modulo techniques: there is, in fact, a limited range at any instant within which the ordinal numbers may vary. We shall only discuss the basic algorithm, after having discussed Ricart and Agrawala's approach, because in fact the two suggestions use the same algorithm, although their terminology sometimes differs.

RICART AND AGRAWALA'S APPROACH

In their reply to Carvalho and Roucairol's algorithm, Ricart and Agrawala (1983) made a new proposal, which is found to be the same as Suzuki and Kasami's.

Their analytic viewpoint is, however, very different: it is based on the definition of a 'symmetric distributed algorithm'. To them, symmetry means that every process is informed of every new request. If a less restrictive definition is adopted, it is possible, using identical process texts, to reduce the number of messages in the same way as was done by Carvalho and Roucairol's algorithm. Within this algorithm, the process that is in its critical section has a virtual token, representing its privileged status; it can keep returning to its critical section for as long as it holds that token, without consulting the other processes.

Ricart and Agrawala's new algorithm makes this token explicit, with processes transmitting it to each other in accordance with their requests. The token is initially assigned to a process selected at random. Unlike the case where the token remains implicit, here, because it is explicit, it must be held at any instant by some process or another, whether or not that process is attempting to enter its critical section. Note that this leads to the possible problem of loss of the token.

THE BASIS OF SUZUKI AND KASAMI'S OR RICART AND AGRAWALA'S ALGORITHM

The token is requested by process P_i using a timestamped request message broadcast to all other processes — P_i does not know which process has the token. The token contains the serial number or timestamp of the last visit it made to each of the P_k processes. Once process P_j, which holds the token, no longer wishes to use it to access its critical section, it looks for the first process P_k (k in the order $j + 1$, ..., n, 1, ... $j - 1$) such that the timestamp of the last request from P_k is greater than the timestamp stored on the token during its last visit to P_k.

THE ALGORITHM

Process P_i has the following declarations:

> *var osn* : 1 .. + ∞
> *tokenpresent* : *boolean* ;
> *inside* : *boolean* ;
> *token* : **array** [1 .. *n*] *of* 0 .. + ∞;
> *requests* : **array** [1 .. *n*] *of* 0 .. + ∞;

The *wait* (*tkn*, *token*) operation causes a wait for a *tkn* type message, and places the message received in variable *token*.
The protocol is as follows:

> *if* ¬ *tokenpresent* *then*
>   *begin*
>   *osn* ← *osn* + 1;
>   *broadcast* (*req*, *osn*, *i*);
>   *wait* (*tkn*, *token*);
>   *end* ;
> *endif* ;
> *inside* ← *true* ;
> *tokenpresent* ← *true* ;
> < *critical section* >;
> *token* [*i*] ← *osn* ;
> *inside* ← *false* ;
> *for j* = *i* + 1 *to n step* 1,
>   = 1 *to i* − 1 *step* 1 *do*
>   *if* (*request* [*j*] > *token* [*j*]) ∧ *tokenpresent*
>   *then begin*
>   *tokenpresent* ← *false* ;
>   *send* (*tkn*, token) *to j* ;
>   *end* ;
>   *endif* ;

on receipt
  of (*req*, *k*, *j*) *do*
        begin
              request [*j*] ← *max* (*request* [*j*], *k*);
if tokenpresent ∧ ⌐ *inside*
                    then < *identical text to the postlude* >
              endif;
              end;

Comment

We shall leave it to the reader to check that this algorithm guarantees mutual exclusion (the number of variables *tokenpresent* = *true* cannot exceed 1) and avoids deadlock. It is also fair, if messages are delivered within a finite time: execution of the postlude transmits the token to the first process P_k ($k = i + 1$, $i + 2,..$, n, 1, ... $i - 1$) whose request message has reached P_i. The length of the delay cannot be quantified unless we know the maximum message transfer time. From the point of view of starvation, this algorithm resembles Dekker's (Dijkstra 1965a; cf. Section 2.1): here, fairness depends on the message transport system's 'fairness' (all messages must be delivered within a finite time), just as in Dekker's algorithm it depends on the lower level — the hardware's fairness.

NUMBER AND SIZE OF MESSAGES

The number of messages required by this algorithm for mutual exclusion is either n [$(n - 1)$ to broadcast the request, and 1 to bring the token representing privileged status to the requesting process] or none (if the process already has the token and wants to re-enter its critical section).

So far as the number of messages needed is concerned, this is therefore a very good algorithm. On the other hand, the size of messages carried is not the same as in the other algorithms. In the others, a message was made up of its type and a timestamp, but this is only the case here for the request messages, while the message carrying the token is made up of an array of n timestamps.

THE USE OF TIMESTAMPS

This algorithm makes no allowance for resetting the timestamping clocks *osn* with respect to each other. For a given process, P_i for example, *osn* is only used to update, on the one hand, *request* [*i*] variables in the other processes by way of *req* type messages, and, on the other hand, *token* [*i*] variables, when messages of the *tkn* type are transferred. Clocks are not therefore used here, as they were in Ricart and Agrawala's (1981) or Lamport's algorithm, to provide for timing of requests in such a way as to impose a total ordering on them. Clocks are only used to time requests issued by a given site in order to be able to compare the time of the last request issued and that of the last time it was granted mutual exclusion, with respect to all the other processes P_i, so as to be sure that the token is properly transmitted from process to process. Moreover, the value *token* [i] contained in the token message indicates the number of times exclusion has been granted to a process P_i.

The authors therefore are applying a wholly different philosophy here, both to algorithm design and to the use of clocks.

5.7. Another timestamping system: the acceptance threshold

Carvalho and Roucairol (1982) have also studied the distribution of an assertion, and propose a systematic process for deriving distributed algorithms from such an assertion. These issues are taken up again and analysed in greater depth in Carvalho and Roucairol (1983b).

THE CONCEPT OF A MIN-MAX LIMIT PAIR

A fundamental concept, for this proposal, is that of a 'min-max limit pair'. Such a pair is based on two variables x_1 and x_2 which vary over the same partially ordered set of values and are related by the assertion $x_1 \leqslant x_2$. In the study of distributed systems, a possible interpretation for this pair would be, for example, to consider x_1 as the knowledge that a site P_1 has of the circumstances of a site P_2, or vice versa.

The need to preserve the assertion $x_1 \leqslant x_2$ means that we have to define rules that allow for x_1 and x_2 to vary in such a way as to respect this constraint. If both variables are on the same site, there is no difficulty in defining these rules. If, on the other hand, they are on different sites, any change in the value of x_1 by the site on which it is located must obey the following rule: the site on which x_2 is located must give its authority to any such change; the same naturally applies to changes in the value of x_2. These considerations led to the concept of the acceptance threshold.

ACCEPTANCE THRESHOLD

An acceptance threshold *at* [j] affects the relations of a process P_i with another process P_j — it is a clock local to P_i that makes it possible to timestamp messages that P_i sends to P_j.

Therefore, for a network of processes P_1, ..., P_i, ..., P_n, unlike the algorithms proposed by Lamport, Ricart and Agrawala (1981 version) or

Carvalho and Roucairol (1981-1983 versions), there is no 'global' timestamping mechanism by which local clocks are reset with respect to each other when messages are transferred.

Such a global mechanism is replaced by a set of 'bi-local' mechanisms, i.e. mechanisms that each involve just two sites. A clock operating on such a mechanism is called an acceptance threshold. In cases involving n processes there are therefore $n(n - 1)$ acceptance thresholds, where before there were only n local clocks. One advantage of the new method is that it is based on greater distribution of the timing mechanism, which may make it more fault-tolerant.

The term 'acceptance threshold' is derived from the use of this timing mechanism to govern modifications in variables involved in a min-max pair expressing a relation between variables from two processes.

Threshold $at [j]$ takes monotonically increasing values which, as we pointed out earlier, timestamp messages sent by P_i towards P_j. Variable x_1 may be changed to x'_1 by P_i so that $x_1 \leqslant x_2$ no longer holds, if and only if P_i has received from P_j — the site managing x_2 — a message stamped k carrying a value x'_2 such that:

(1) $k > at [j]$
(2) $x'_2 \geqslant max (x'_1, x_1)$

In other words, x_1 may not increase to x'_1 until P_i has received a message indicating that P_j has previously (in a sense defined by causality relations, i.e. the total ordering of events in the two processes P_i and P_j) incremented x_2 and x'_2. An analogous rule applies to the modification of x_2 by P_j if this modification would invalidate $x_1 \leqslant x_2$, i.e. if x_2 is being decremented.

What makes this rule systematic is the fact that whenever P_i decrements x_1, it informs P_j of the fact, and P_j does the same whenever it increments x_2. Other modifications to x_1 can only take place once these messages have been received.

As well as these concepts, the authors propose a transformation system for variables involved in an assertion, which they elaborate in the course of deriving distributed algorithms taking that assertion as their starting point. This makes it possible to obtain variables characterizing the state of processes and related to each other in min-max pairs. The interested reader should refer to Carvalho and Roucairol (1983b) for further details.

A MUTUAL EXCLUSION ALGORITHM

In Carvalho and Roucairol (1983b), the authors describe two algorithms, one of which implements mutual exclusion between two processes, while the other allows at most two processes out of three to enter a particular section of code.

We shall here present the basis of an algorithm for mutual exclusion between

n processes founded on the principles we have just been discussing. It is interesting to note that this algorithm resembles the other algorithms proposed by the same authors (Carvalho and Roucairol 1983a), which we were discussing in Section 5.5, from the point of view of its structure and of the number of messages it requires to implement exclusion: the intuitive and systematic approaches lead to the same goals.

The basic principle of the algorithm can be broken down into two parts. We shall start by examining the timestamping mechanism. Every process P_i contains an array at $[1 .. n]$ such that at $[j]$ is the acceptance threshold for P_i with respect to P_j: P_i will accept no message from P_j unless its timestamp is greater than at $[j]$. At any moment at $[j]$ is equal to the highest value the timestamp on messages between P_i and P_j has reached. Every process has a variable hsn such that at any moment $hsn = max$ $(at$ $[j])$; this variable makes it possible to timestamp messages sent by P_i to any other process P_k, and we then have at $[k] = hsn$.

The second part of the algorithm concerns the handling of variables controlling entry into critical sections. Every process has an array *perm* $[1 .. n]$: when all its elements are true, P_i may enter its critical section. This array is handled in exactly the same way as the one discussed in Section 5.5, to which we refer the reader.

Chapter 6

Two further control problems

6.1. Introduction

In Chapter 2 we examined a number of algorithms implementing mutual exclusion for access to a critical section. The fundamental characteristic of all these algorithms was that they were not based on any predefined synchronization mechanism: they used only memory read or write instructions to guarantee the desired properties. In this chapter we tackle two new problems and describe algorithms, based on the same assumptions, to solve them: these are the producer-consumer and reader-writer problems. The reasons for studying these algorithms applied to the two problems lay not merely in mental gymnastics designed to improve our understanding of the *problems*, but in deriving *solutions* that either demonstrate a methodology (the producer-consumer case) or have certain interesting properties not shown by traditional solutions based on specialized synchronization tools (the reader-writer case).

6.2. The producer-consumer problem

STATEMENT OF THE PROBLEM

The producer-consumer problem is very simple. A process, which we shall call the producer, sends messages to another process, the consumer. The messages produced but not yet consumed are stored in a memory, which we shall call a buffer. There is a fixed number of buffers, n, and they are used in a circular way: a buffer whose contents have been consumed may be reused.

Two procedures are provided for producer and consumer processes, to place messages in the buffer or withdraw them from it: *produce* and *consume*. Execution of these procedures must be synchronized in such a way that messages produced cannot be consumed more than once (the consumer cannot 'overtake' the producer), no message can be lost through overloading a buffer (producers cannot 'lap' consumers), and messages are consumed in the order in which they are produced.

In order to give a formal specification of these constraints, we shall use control module language (Robert and Verjus 1977, Raynal 1983). This language defines a certain number of event counters for each procedure whose execution must be monitored. We shall be using the following:

\# *auth* (*p*) = number of times that procedure *p* has been allowed to execute.
\# *term* (*p*) = number of complete executions of procedure *p*.

With these counters, we can give the conditions governing the execution of procedures *produce* and *consume*.

condition (*produce*) : \# *auth* (*produce*) — \# *term* (*consume*) < *n*
condition (*consume*) : \# *term* (*produce*) — \# *auth* (*consume*) > 0

SOLUTION 1

This solution involves translating the abstract specification given above, using four variables of the language in which the solution is programmed to represent the four counters that it uses (Andrea et al. 1985). We then obtain the following declarations, which are global for the two processes (the producer and the consumer), and which may be divided into two groups: declarations concerned with procedure control and declarations concerned with the buffer or its management.

var *inum beg prod, num end prod,*
    num beg cons, num end cons : 0 .. + ∞;
    buffer : **array** 0 .. *n* − 1 *of message* ;
    in, out : 0 .. *n* − 1;

The control variables are initialized to 0; *in* and *out*, which are also initialized to 0, are *buffer* pointers: *buffer* [*in*] and *buffer* [*out*] give the next empty or full buffer location, respectively.

Procedures *produce* and *consume* are constructed along the same lines:

    (1) — wait for condition
    (2) — update variable \# *auth* (*p*)
    (3) — action on the buffer
    (4) — update variable \# *term* (*p*).

No synchronization primitive of the semaphore (Dijkstra 1965) or monitor (Hoare 1974) type is therefore used to protect access to global variables.

procedure *produce* (*m* : *message*);
    begin
        wait *num beg prod* − *num end cons* < *n* ;
        num beg prod ← *num beg prod* + 1;
        buffer [*in*] ← *m* ;
        in ← *in* + 1 **mod** *n* ;

```
        num end prod ← num end prod + 1;
    end;
procedure consume (m : message);
    begin
        wait num beg cons – num end prod < 0;
        num beg cons ← num beg cons + 1;
        m ← buffer out;
        out ← out + 1 mod n; num end cons ← num end cons + 1;
    end;
```

No mutual exclusion is provided for the state variables used, other than what is offered by the hardware itself to govern read and write instructions. The validity of this solution is based on the fact that, on the one hand, the state variables, which are tested in the wait statement, are monotonically increasing and, on the other hand, the sign of the coefficient that assigns them 'goes towards' inequality in the conditions. These aspects, called 'regularity', are studied in Bochman (1979) and generalized in Herman (1981). Note, finally, that depending on the language in which this solution is programmed, it may be possible to declare variables and define both procedures within a single program structuring unit (module or abstract type), which will ensure that the solution is modular (Wegner and Smolka 1983). Andrea et al. (1985) uses a methodical approach to show that if instead of using state variables to give the state of processes with respect to the buffer, the state of the buffer were defined using two variables:

$$full = \# \ term \ (produce) - \# \ auth \ (consume)$$
$$empty = N + \# \ term \ (consume) - \# \ end \ (produce)$$

it becomes necessary to allow for mutual exclusion between the modifications to variables if the solution is to be consistent (the variables are no longer monotonically increasing).

SOLUTION 2

Another solution to this problem is proposed in Peterson and Silberschatz (1983). The variables used, which are global for the two processes, are:

```
var buffer : array [0 .. n – 1] of message;
    in, out : 0 .. n – 1;
```

in and *out*, initialized to 0, show the next free and next occupied message in *buffer* respectively.

Noting that the buffer is full (and therefore we cannot produce) when $in + 1$ *mod* $n = out$, and that it is empty (so we cannot consume), when $in = out$, we obtain the following procedure:

procedure (*produce*) (*m* : *message*);
    begin
        wait (*in* + 1 **mod** *n* ≠ *out*);
        buffer [*in*] ← *m* ;
        in ← *in* + 1 **mod** *n* ;
    end ;
procedure consume (*m* : *message*);
    begin
        wait *in* ≠ *out* ;
        m ← *buffer* [*out*];
        out ← *out* + 1 **mod** *n* ;
    end ;

This solution, although it is based on a less methodical approach than the preceding one, is in fact equivalent to it. It can be obtained from the preceding one by eliminating the state variables concerning control, which are operationally redundant given that we are using input and output pointers.

We shall now examine another problem, which is more difficult to solve without using synchronization primitives, the reader-writer problem.

6.3. Another reader-writer problem

STATEMENT OF THE PROBLEM

This problem was first posed by Courtois et al. (1971). Consider $n + 1$ processes sharing a data set. Amongst these processes, n can read these data at the same time; these are the readers. The remaining process may change the values of the data; this is the writer.

In cases where the data set can be held in a single memory location there is no control problem: the mutual exclusion provided by the hardware makes any protocol unnecessary, as reading or writing a memory location are both atomic operations. This is no longer the case if the shared data set cannot be reduced to a single location, and if the operations are only atomic with respect to one data item at a time. We then need to construct an algorithm that will guarantee the consistency of the whole data set: readers will obtain correct and recent data, the writer can modify them. The rules to respect if this consistency is to be guaranteed are that readers and the writer mutually exclude each other, while all readers may read data simultaneously. In cases where there are several writers, they are all mutually exclusive.

A CLASSIC SOLUTION: SEMAPHORES

Solutions to this problem are provided in many texts on operating systems. We shall briefly mention a traditional form of solution which uses semaphores. A semaphore *mutex* initialized to 1 guarantees that access for writing is exclusive. It is used by the writer before and after writing, and is also used by the first reader, in order to find out if a writer is currently writing data, and by the last reader, in order to release readers from their exclusion by the writer. A counter *numread* counts the number of readers, and a semaphore *mutread* (initialized to n) is responsible for its consistency.

The variables necessary are therefore:

> *var mutex, mutread, semaphore*;
> *numread* : $0 .. + \infty$;

and reading and writing procedures are as follows:

> *procedure* write (x : *data*);
>   *begin*
>   P (*mutex*);
>   < write data x >;
>   V (*mutex*);
>   *end*;
> *procedure* read (x : *data*);
>   *begin*
>   P (*mutread*);
>   *numread* ← *numread* + 1;
>   *if numread* = 1 *then* P (*mutex*) *endif;*
>   V (*mutread*);
>   < read the data in x >;
>   P (*mutread*);
>   *numread* ← *numread* − 1;
>   *if numread* = 0 *then* V (*mutex*) *endif*;
>   V (*mutread*);
>   *end*;

There are many solutions to this problem, and they are more or less easy to design or to understand depending on the properties of the language in which they are presented. Solutions have been proposed based on monitors (Hoare 1974), critical regions (Brinch Hansen 1972), control modules (Robert and Verjus 1977), or the Ada language (Le Verrand 1985).

Note that the solution proposed here will not avoid starvation for writers, whether the number of readers is finite or not. This means that a different algorithm must be proposed depending on whether we want to give readers or writers priority, or to have no priority at all (the fair solution).

PETERSON'S PROBLEM

The problem proposed by Peterson (1983b) assumes that there are n readers and a single writer. The requirement is to find a solution to this problem that does not use synchronization primitives or specialized instructions, and such that read and write operations can take place concurrently (what Peterson called the 'Concurrent Reading While Writing Problem'). The ultimate aim is to find a solution that also avoids processes having to wait; under such conditons access to data is no longer serialized, and as waiting is eliminated — and with it any solution based on mutual exclusion — parallelism is maximized. Read operations have, of course, to return the latest value written. This problem has also been studied by Lamport (1977), but his assumptions were less strict — the writer never has to wait, starvation of readers is possible.

We shall derive the solution by successive approximations. The first lays down the general framework of the problem and proposes a 'traditional' solution based on exclusion primitives; the second will, in fact, be Lamport's algorithm; the third will be the solution we are looking for. In adopting this approach, we are following Peterson's presentation.

TRADITIONAL SOLUTION BASED ON MUTUAL EXCLUSION

This solution uses distributed Boolean variables; one of which is accessible for reading by any process but is accessible for writing by only one of them.

> *var writing* : *boolean* ;
>   *reading* : **array** [1 .. n] **of** *boolean* ;

These Booleans, which are initialized to false, are used to indicate the state of processes with respect to the shared data. The mutual exclusion protocol for the critical section is guaranteed by procedures *prelude* $(i, n + 1)$ and *postlude* $(i, n + 1)$ used respectively to enter and to exit the critical section; i is the number of process and $(n + 1)$ is the total number of processes.

The protocols are as follows, where processes $P_1, ..., P_i, ..., P_n$ are readers, and P_{n-1} is the writer.

For a reader P_i:

> **procedure** *read* $(i : 1 .. n, x : data)$;
>   **begin**
>   *prelude* $(i, n + 1)$;
>   **wait** *writing* = *false* ;
>   *reading* [i] ← *true* ;
>   *postlude* $(i, n + 1)$;
>   < *read* : *x* ← *data* >;
>   *reading* [i] ← *false* ;
>   **end** ;

For the writer P_{n-1}:

> **procedure** *write* $(x : data)$;
>   **begin**
>   *prelude* $(n + 1, n + 1)$;

> *wait* $\forall\, j \in 1 \,..\, n$: *reading* $[j] = false$;
> *writing* $\leftarrow$ *false* ;
> *postlude* $(n + 1, n + 1)$;
> $<$ *write date* $>$;
>   *end* ;

This solution allows for parallelism between readers and can easily be generalized to cases where there are *m* writers. We then obtain a solution to the traditional reader-writer problem. The fairness of this solution depends on the fairness of the exclusion algorithm used.

Note that the solution has been built around a 'prevention' technique: processes are blocked for as long as the state of the system does not allow them to advance.

SECOND SOLUTION: AN ALGORITHM ALONG THE LINES OF LAMPORT (1977)

Instead of a preventive approach as above, we could go for a 'cure' technique, in which each process is allowed to execute and if the result is unsatisfactory, has to start again. This is the attitude adopted in Lamport's 1977 algorithm. The writer — remember that we have assumed that there is only one — may always execute, giving new values to the data.

Readers, on the other hand, may obtain results produced by two different write operations: under such conditions they must start reading again. Clearly, this means that there can be reader starvation.

Defining the necessary protocols requires very detailed examination of all the cases that may occur:

(1) The writer uses a Boolean *rflag* to indicate that it is writing data. Readers test the variable *rflag* before and after reading to determine whether its read operation has overlapped with writing.

(2) Writing may have taken place entirely in the space of a single read operation. To determine whether this is the case a Boolean variable *switch* is reversed at each write operation.

(3) Now we are left with the problem of two or more write operations that may have taken place in the course of a single read operation. To deal with this case, we need a pair of Booleans for each reader P_i : *rd* [*i*] is used by the reader, *wr* [*i*] by the writer. The reader sets them to different values, while the writer makes them equal.

With all this information, a reader can discover whether a read operation has overlapped with a write operation, wholly or in part, or with several write operations. In any of these cases, it repeats its operations.

The variables shared by all the processes are initialized to false. They are:

> *var rflag* : *boolean* ;
>   *switch* : *boolean* ;

          wr, rd : **array** [1 .. *n*] *of boolean* ;

Every reader has two local variables, *sswitch* and *sflag*, which it uses to store the values of *switch* and *rflag* before reading.

Protocol for reader P_i :

```
procedure read (i : 1 .. n, x : data);
    repeat
        rd [i] ← ⌐ wr [i];
        repeat
            sflag ← rflag ;
            sswitch ← switch ;
            < read : x ← data >;
        until ⌐ [sflag ∨ rflag ∨ (sswitch ≠ switch)];
    until rd [i] ≠ wr [i];
```

The internal loop provides for the process to wait in cases such as 1 and 2 above, while the external loop is used for case 3.

Protocol for the writer P_{n-1} :

```
procedure write (x : data);
        begin
        rflag ← true ;
        < write data x >;
        switch ← ⌐ switch ;
        rflag ← false ;
        for j = 1 to n do
            if rd [i] ≠ wr [i]
                then wr [i] ← rd [i]
            endif ;
    end ;
```

Boolean values are modified in such a way as to cause readers to repeat operations where necessary to obtain correct values.

It is obvious that a single buffer is needed to contain the data read by P_1, ..., P_n and written by P_{n-1}. We shall see that this is no longer the case if the solution is to avoid any kind of waiting — which, in a manner of speaking, means that all processes have priority.

PETERSON'S ALGORITHM

Peterson proposes a solution in which none of the processes wait, so starvation is avoided. The text of the protocols is a series of statements without branching or repetition.

The solution proposed meets all the requirements of the problem posed (the CRWW problem). It is based on the last algorithm and takes advantage of the possibility of making copies of all shared data: $(n + 2)$ buffers are then necessary to store the required number of copies of shared data. Peterson shows that this number is both necessary and sufficient to resolve the problem under circumstances where we have no other information on the data.

Booleans *rflag*, *switch* and the pair (*rd* [*i*], *wr* [*i*]) are used, as before, to protect a buffer containing the data: *buffer* 1. This is the buffer that provides readers with correct data while the writer is not modifying it. A second buffer, *buffer* 2, is used as a kind of 'backup copy'. For every reader P_i, there is a buffer *buff* [*i*] that the writer uses to provide [*i*]*P* with a backup copy of data for use in cases of concurrent reading and writing. The pair (*rd* [*i*], *wr* [*i*]) is also used to indicate that a copy has been put in *buff* [*i*].

The basic protocol used by the writer is to write data first in *buffer* 1, then to make a copy in *buff* [*i*] for each of the readers whose execution overlaps with its own, and finally to make another copy in *buffer* 2. This sequence of operations by the writer is very similar to what occurs in the last algorithm, but with the addition of the update operation of the copies held in *buff* [*j*] and *buffer* 2.

Protocol for the writer:

```
procedure write (x : data);
    begin
        rflag ← true;
        < write x in buffer 1 >;
        switch ← ⌐ switch;
        rflag ← false;
        for j = 1 to n do
            if rd [j] ≠ wr [j]
                then begin
                    < write x in buff [j] >;
                    wr [j] ← rd [j];
                    end;
            endif;
        < write x in buffer 2>;
    end;
```

The protocol for reader P_i is to read *buffer* 1 first, then the 'backup copy' *buffer* 2. P_i then checks whether a copy of *buff* [*i*] has been made (by testing whether *rd* [*i*] = *wr* [*i*]) and if this is the case, it returns the data given in that copy. If such a copy has not been made, it gives the value *d1* of the data previously read in *buffer* 1 if it is correct — which it determines using the Boolean indicators — and the value *d2* read in *buffer* 2 otherwise.

This protocol therefore has points in common with the previous one, in particular the way indicators are used to determine whether or not the data contained in *buffer* 1 are correct.

Protocol for reader P_i:

```
procedure read (i : 1 .. n, x : data);
```

```
begin
    rd [i] ← wr [i];
    sflag ← rflag;
    sswitch ← switch;
    < read : d1 data from buffer 1 >;
    sflag 2 ← rflag;
    sswitch 2 ← switch;
    <read : d2 ← data from buffer 2>;
    d1 incorrect ← (sswitch ≠ sswitch 2) ∨ sflag ∨ sflag 2;
if rd [i] = wr [i] then  < read : x ← buff [i] >
elsif d1 incorrect then  < read : x ← d2 >
                    else < read : x ← d1 >
    endif;
end;
```

PROOF

Two points have to be proved: the consistency of the value returned at the end of reading, and a guarantee that the value read is the most recent.

As far as the first point is concerned, we need only note that if the execution of the writer's operations overlaps with those of a reader who was reading *buffer* 2, it will in the meanwhile have made a copy of the data in *buff* $[i]$, between writing to these two buffers. The readers will therefore obtain a correct value (see Peterson 1983b).

We can reach the same conclusion by reasoning in terms of specific cases. Whether or not the reading of *buffer* 1 is correct is determined using $d1$ *incorrect*, and the pair $(rd [i], wr [i])$ is used in the same way for *buff* $[i]$.

There is, however, no Boolean guard for reading *buffer* 2. We must therefore make sure that if the writing of *buffer* 2 and its reading by P_i have interferred with each other, P_i will not return $d2$ as a result, i.e. under those conditions either $d1$ or *buff* $[i]$ must be correct. There are two possible cases. If $d1$ *incorrect* = false, then it is self-evident that the value of the data $d1$ is correct and should be returned as a result; otherwise, reading by P_i and writing to *buffer* 1 have interfered, and as there has also been interference on *buffer* 2 (under our assumptions), the writer will necessarily find $rd [i] \neq wr [i]$ and will therefore make a copy of the data in *buff* $[i]$ and indicate the fact by setting $wr [i] ← rd [i]$. The reader P_i will become aware of this fact after reading *buffer* 2, and will then return the correct value *buff* $[i]$.

It still remains to be shown that the value obtained on reading will be the most recent. If the value of data returned as a result is *buff* $[i]$, this means that reading and writing were concurrent and therefore that the value was the most recent possible. If the value returned is obtained from *buffer* 1, it is obvious that it is the most recently written because it is the first buffer written by the writer. The only problem that can arise is when the reader obtains the most recent value from *buffer* 1 or *buff* [*i*], but returns less recent results from *buffer* 2. Taking into account that the reader returns the value *d*2 from *buffer* 2 as a result only if *d*1 is incorrect, this means that under these conditions the writer has begun to write new values once more and therefore at that moment the value *d*2 is the most recent.

OTHER PROBLEMS, OTHER SOLUTIONS

After discussing the solution we have just described, Peterson (1983b) goes on to examine some variants of the problem he posed. Priority for the writer — it must never have to wait — is a constant constraint to be met, but the behaviour of readers may differ.

In variant 1, only the writer may cause readers to wait. The solution is essentially the same as the previous one without *buffer* 2; a reader P_i will repeat its reading operation under conditions where in the previous algorithm it would have returned *d*2 as a result. The read operation will keep on being repeated until the writer has finished writing *buffer* 1 or *buff* [*i*]. This solution is fair: there can be no starvation for readers because the writer cannot modify *buffer* 1 twice in succession without having made a copy in *buff* [*i*] in the meantime. This is the fundamental difference from the 'Lamport-style' algorithm we discussed before. Peterson shows that $n + 1$ buffers are necessary and sufficient to solve this problem.

In variant 2, a reader cannot be made to wait by the writer but only by other readers. A mutual exclusion protocol ensures that only one process at a time can carry out a read operation. The protocol for a reader is the same as the one we saw above, but with a prelude and postlude section to handle mutual exclusion. The protocol for the writer is exactly the same. Because of mutual exclusion between readers, it is exactly as if there were only one reader, and therefore only three buffers are necessary and sufficient to solve the problem. Fairness between readers depends on the fairness of the mutual exclusion mechanism used.

These variants are of considerable interest from the point of view of algorithm research because of their implications for parallelism and its control, and, above all, for their attempt to maximize parallelism. It is also worth noting that, all other things being equal, the number of buffers needed becomes constant as soon as one allows significant waiting within the mutual exclusion mechanism.

To conclude, we shall simply point out that Peterson's algorithm also has an interesting qualitative consequence: control of concurrency does not always require mutual exclusion, whether it depends on specialized primitives or is built on software techniques such as those discussed in Chapter 2.

References

ALFORD D.W., ANSART J.P., HAMMEL G., LAMPORT L., LISKOV B., MULLERY G.P. and SCHNEIDER F.B. (1985): *Distributed Systems*; *LNCS* (190) Springer Verlag, 574 pp.

AMBLER A.L. et al. (1977): GYPSY: A language for specification and implementation of verifiable programs; *Proc. ACM. Conf. on LDRS*, Sigplan Notices, **12** (3), 1-10.

ANDRE F., HERMAN D. and VERJUS J.P. (1985): *Synchronization of Parallel Programs*; North Oxford Academic, Oxford, 110pp.

BALZER R.M. (1971): PORTS: A method for dynamic interprogram communications and job control; *AFIPS Conf. Proc.*, **38**, SJCC, 485-489.

BOCHMAN G.V. (1979): Distributed synchronization and regularity; *Computer Networks*, **3**, 36-43.

BRINCH HANSEN P. (1972): A comparison of two synchronizing concepts; *Acta Informatica*, **1** (3), 190-199.

BRINCH HANSEN P. (1973): *Operating System Principles*; Prentice Hall, New Jersey.

BRINCH HANSEN P. (1975): The programming language Concurrent Pascal; *IEEE Trans. on Software Engineering* **SE1**, 199-207.

BRINCH HANSEN P. (1978): Distributed processes: a concurrent programming concept; *Comm. ACM*, **2** (11), 934-941.

BURNS J.E., (1981): Symmetry in systems of asynchronous processes; *Proc. 22nd Annual Symp. on Foundations of Computer Science*, 169-174.

BURNS J.E. and LYNCH N.A. (1980): Mutual exclusion using indivisible reads and writes; *Proc. 18th Annual Allerton Conf. on Communications, Control and Computing*, 833-842.

BURNS J.E. et al. (1982): Data requirements for implementation of n-process mutual exclusion using a single shared variable; *Journal of ACM*, **29** (1), 183-205.

CARVALHO O. and ROUCAIROL G. (1981): Une amélioration de l'algorithme d'exclusion mutuelle de Ricart et Agrawala; *Rapport de recherche no. 81-58:* LITP, Paris 7.

CARVALHO O. and ROUCAIROL G. (1982): On the distribution of assertion; *Proc. of ACM-SIGACT-SIGOPS Symp. on Principles of Distributed Computing*. Ottawa, pp. 121-131.

CARVALHO O. and ROUCAIROL G. (1983a): On mutual exclusion in computer networks; *Comm. ACM* **26** (2), 146-147.

CARVALHO O. and ROUCAIROL G. (1983b): Assertion, decomposition and partial correctness of distributed control algorithms; in *Distributed Computing Systems*, Paker and Verjus (Eds); Academic Press, pp. 67-93.

CARVER HILL J. (1973): Synchronizing processor with memory-content-generated interrupts; *Comm ACM*, **16** (6), 350-351.

CONWAY M.E. (1963): Design of a separable transition diagram compiler; *Comm. ACM*, **6** (7), 396-408.

CORNAFION (collective name) (1981): *Systèmes informatiques répartis;* Dunod, 367 pp.

COURTOIS P.J., HEYMANS F. and PARNAS D.L. (1971): Concurrent control with readers and writers; *Comm. ACM*, **14** (10), 667-668.

CROCUS (collective name) (1975): *Systemes d'exploitation des ordinateurs;* Dunod, 364 pp.

DAHL O.J., DIJKSTRA E.W. and HOARE C.A.R. (1972): *Structured Programming*; Academic Press, London, 220 pp.

DE BRUIJN J.G. (1967): Additional comments on a problem in concurrent programming control; *Comm. ACM* **10** (3), 137-138.

DIJKSTRA E.W. (1965): Co-operating sequential processes; in *Programming Languages*, F. Genuys (Eds); Academic Press, New York, pp. 43-112.

DIJKSTRA E.W. (1968): The structure of the multiprogramming system; *Comm. ACM* **11** (5), 341-346.

DIJKSTRA E.W. (1971): Hierarchical ordering of sequential processes; *Acta Informatica*, **1** (2), 115-138.

DIJKSTRA E.W. (1974): Self-stabilizing systems in spite of distributed control; *Comm. ACM*, **17** (11), 643-644.

DORAN R.W. and THOMAS L.K. (1980): Variants of the software solution to mutual exclusion; *Inf. Proc. Lett.* **10** (4), 206-208.

EISENBERG M.A. and McGUIRE M.R. (1972): Further comments on Dijkstra's concurrent programming control problem; *Comm. ACM*, **15** (11), and 999.

ESWARAN K.P., GRAY J.N., LORIE R. and TRAIGER L.L. (1976): The notion of consistency and predicate locks in a data base system; *Comm. ACM*, **19** (11), 624-633.

GOTTLIEB A., LUBACHEVSKY B.D. and RUDOLPH L. (1983): Basic techniques for the efficient coordination of very large numbers of cooperating sequential processors; *ACM Toplas*, **5** (2), 164-189.

HABERMAN A.N. (1972): Synchronization of communication processes; *Comm. ACM*, **15** (3), 171-176.

HABERMAN A.N. (1976): *Introduction to Operating System Design*; Science Research Associates, Palo Alto.

HEHNER E.C.R. and SHYAMASUNDAR R.K. (1981): An implementation of P and V; *Inf. Proc. Lett.*, **12** *(4)*, 196-198.

HERMAN D. (1981): Controle réparti des synchronisations entre processus; *Proc. of the 2nd Int. Conf. on Distributed Computing*, Paris, pp. 24-30.

HOARE C.A.R. (1972): Towards a theory of parallel programming; in *DS Techniques* Hoare and Perrott (Eds), Academic Press.

HOARE C.A.R. (1974): Monitor: an operating system structuring concept; *Comm. ACM*, 17 (10), 549-557, Corrigendum in *Comm. ACM*, **18** (2), 95, (1975).

HOARE C.A.R. (1978): Communicating sequential processes; *Comm. ACM*, **21** (8), 666-677.

HORNING J.J. and RANDELL B. (1973): Process structuring; *Computing Surveys*, **5** (1), 5-30.

HYMAN H. (1966): Comments on a problem in concurrent programming control; *Comm. ACM*, **9** (1), 45.

ICHBIAH J. et al. (1983): *Reference Manual for the ADA Programming Language*; ANSI/MIL-STD 1815 A.

KANEKO A., NISHIHARA Y., TSURVOKA K. and HATTORI M. (1979): Logical clock synchronization method for duplicated data base control; *Proc. of the Int. Conf. on Distributed Computing Systems*, Huntsville, pp. 601-611.

KESSELS J.L.W. (1977): An alternative to event queue for synchronization in monitors; *Comm. ACM*, **20** (7), 500-503.

KESSELS J.L.W. (1982): Arbitration without common modifiable variables; *Acta Informatica*, **17** 135-141.

KNUTH D.E. (1966): Additional comments on a problem in concurrent programming control; *Comm. ACM*, **9** (5), 321-322.

KOSARAJU S. (1973): Limitations of Dijkstra's semaphores, primitives and Petri nets; *Operating Systems Review*, **7** (4), 122-126.

KRUIJER H.S.M. (1979): Self-stabilization (in spite of distributed control) in tree-structured systems; *Inf. Proc. Lett.*, **8** (2), 91-95.

LAMPORT L. (1974): A new solution of Dijkstra's concurrent programming problem; *Comm. ACM*, **17** (8), 453-455.

LAMPORT L. (1977): Concurrent reading and writing; *Comm. ACM*, **20** (11), 806-811.

LAMPORT L. (1978): Time, clocks and the ordering of events in a distributed system; *Comm. ACM*, **21** (7), 558-565.

LE GUERNIC P. and RAYNAL M. (1980): *L'expression de la communication dans les langages: des analyses et une proposition*; Rapport de Recherche no. 129, IRISA, 84 pp.

LE LANN G. (1977): Distributed systems, towards a formal approach; *IFIP Congress*, Toronto, pp. 155-160.

LE LANN G. (1978): Algorithms for distributed data sharing systems which use tickets; *Proc. of the 3rd Berkeley Workshop on Distributed Data Management and Computer Networks*, pp. 259-272.

LE VERRAND D. (collective name) (1985): *Evaluating Ada*; North Oxford Academic, Oxford, 288 pp.

LISKOV B. et al. (1977): Abstraction mechanism in CLU; *Comm. ACM*, **20** (8), 564-576.

LISTER A.M. (1979): *Fundamentals of Operating Systems*; Macmillan Press.

LISTER A.M. and MAYNARD K.J. (1976): An implementation of monitors; *Software Practice and Experience*, **6** (3), 377-386.

MITCHELL J.G., MAYBURY W. and SWEET R. (1978): *MESA Language Manual*. Report CSL-78-1, Xerox Research Center, Palo Alto.

MORRIS J.M. (1979): A starvation-free solution to the mutual exclusion problem; *Inf. Proc. Lett.* **8** (2), 76-80.

MOSSIERE J., TCHUENTE M. and VERJUS J.P. (1977): *Sur l'exclusion mutuelle dans les réseaux informatiques*; Rapport de Recherche No. 75, IRISA, Rennes, 19pp.

PATIL S. (1971): *Limitations and Capabilities of Dijkstra's Semaphore Primitives for Coordination among Processes*; Technical Report, MIT.

PETERSON L. and SILBERSCHATZ A. (1983): *Operating System Concepts*; Addison-Wesley, 548 pp.

PETERSON G.L. (1981): Myths about the mutual exclusion problem; *Inf. Proc. Lett.*, **12** (3), 115-116.

PETERSON G.L. (1983a): A new solution to Lamport's concurrent programming problem using shared variables; *ACM Toplas*, **5** (1), 56-65.

PETERSON G.L. (1983b): Concurrent reading while writing; *ACM Toplas*, **5** (1), 46-55.

PRESSER L. (1975): Multiprogramming coordination; *Computing Surveys*, **7** (1), 21-44.

RAYNAL M. (1983): An analysis of the specification in interprocess cooperation by means of shared variables; *Technology and Science of Informatics*, **1** (3), 157-166.

RICART G. and AGRAWALA A.K. (1981): An optimal algorithm for mutual exclusion in computer networks; *Comm. ACM*, **24** (1), 9-17. Corrigendum in *Comm. ACM*, **24** (9).

RICART G. and AGRAWALA A.K. (1983): Author's response to 'On mutual exclusion in computer networks' by Carvalho and Roucairol; *Comm. ACM*, **26** (2), 147-148.

RIVEST R.L. and PRATT V.R. (1976): The mutual exclusion problem for unreliable processes: preliminary report; *Proc. of the 17th Annual Symp. on Foundations of Computer Science*, pp. 1-8.

ROBERT P. and VERJUS J.P. (1977): Towards autonomous descriptions of synchronization modules; *IFIP Congress*, Toronto, pp. 981-986.

SCHMIDT H.A. (1976): On the efficient implementation of conditional critical regions and the construction of monitors; *Acta Informatica*, **6**.

SHAW A.C. (1974): *The logical Design of Operating Systems*; Prentice-Hall, New Jersey, 306 pp.

STARK E.W. (1982): Semaphore primitive and starvation-free mutual exclusion; *Journal ACM*, **24** (4), 1049-1072.

SUZUKI I. and KASAMI T. (1982): An optimality theory for mutual exclusion algorithms in computer networks; *Proc. of the 3rd Int. Conf. on Distributed Computing Systems*. Miami, pp. 365-370.

WEGNER P. and SMOLKA S.A. (1983): Processes, tasks and monitors: a comparative study of concurrent programming primitives; *IEEE Trans. on Software Engineering*, **SES9** (4), 446-462.

WIRTH N. (1977): Towards a discipline of real-time programming; *Comm. ACM*, **20** (8), 577-583.

WULF W.A., RUSSEL D.B. and HABERMAN N. (1971): BLISS: a language for system programming; *Comm. ACM*, **14** (2), 780-790.

ZELKOWITZ M. (1971): Interrupt driven programming; *Comm. ACM*, **14** (6), 417-418.

Index

The MIT Press, with Peter Denning as consulting editor, publishes computer science books in the following series:

ACM Doctoral Dissertation Award and Distinguished
 Dissertation Series

Artificial Intelligence, Patrick Winston and Michael Brady,
 editors

Charles Babbage Institute Reprint Series for the History
 of Computing, Martin Campbell-Kelly, editor

Computer Systems, Herb Schwetman, editor

Foundations of Computing, Michael Garey, editor

History of Computing, I. Bernard Cohen and
 William Aspray, editors

Information Systems, Michael Lesk, editor

The MIT Electrical Engineering and Computer Science
 Series

Scientific Computation, Dennis Gannon, editor

For information on submission of manuscripts for
publication, please call or write to:

Frank P. Satlow
Executive Editor
The MIT Press
28 Carleton Street
Cambridge, MA 02142

617/253-1623